LINEBACKER!

LINEBACKER!

George Sullivan

Illustrated with photographs and diagrams

DODD, MEAD & COMPANY   New York

PICTURE CREDITS

Vernon J. Biever, 33; New York Giants, 24, 68; Pro Football Hall of Fame, 17, 19, 20 (right), 21, 25, 26, 28. All other photographs are by George Sullivan.

Frontispiece: **The Bears', Dick Butkus, the pre-eminent linebacker of recent times**

ACKNOWLEDGMENTS

Many persons contributed toward making this book possible. Special thanks are offered the following: Don Weiss, Director of Public Relations, National Football League; Jim Heffernan, Director of Information, National Football Conference; Kay O'Reilly, NFL; Don Smith, Director of Public Relations, Pro Football's Hall of Fame; Ed Croke, New York Giants; Frank Ramos and Jim Trecker, New York Jets; Pat Horne, New England Patriots; Don Phinney, Buffalo Bills; Gary Wagner, Wagner-International Photos; and Herb Field, Herb Field Art Studio.

CONTENTS

Miami Dolphins show classic 4-3 alignment in defensing against the New York Jets.

WHAT IT TAKES

It is second down for the Steelers against the Chiefs. Pittsburgh quarterback Terry Bradshaw calls a sweep. Guards Sam Davis and Bruce Van Dyke lead running back Franco Harris around the left side. The road ahead is clear except for Willie Lanier who is thundering across the field from his position at middle linebacker.

Lanier grabs Van Dyke and flings him to one side, then raises up and crashes both forearms down on Davis' shoulders. Stripped of his blocking, Harris tries to veer to his left. Lanier is too quick. His powerful arms encircle Harris' waist and he pulls him to the ground. The play gains a yard or so.

Lanier hasn't done anything special, only what he's paid to do. Like any linebacker, Lanier must charge into the line and plug holes on slants, plunges, and draws. He must dart back to protect against passes. Or, as it's often said, a linebacker has only one thing to do: everything.

There is no position on defense more important than that of linebacker. "Everyone knows that championships are won by defenses," says Harland Svare, former coach of the San Diego Chargers. "But I go farther. Defenses are made by linebackers. If I were building a football team from scratch, I'd start with the linebackers."

Linebacking is the newest position in pro football. Twenty or thirty years ago, while there were players who backed up the line, covering for the mistakes of their colleagues, the term linebacker hadn't even been invented. But nowadays linebackers like Willie Lanier, Mike Curtis of the Colts, and Nick Buoniconti of the Dolphins are as well known as their teams' quarterbacks, and sometimes even better known.

Not just linebackers, but defensive football, in general, has come into prominence in recent years. It used to be that the same player played "both ways," that is, on offense *and* defense. That policy has gone the way of cardboard shoulder pads and two-legged goal posts. Now each team has a defensive unit staffed by specialists.

Every time the ball is put in play (except in the case of kicks), the defensive players have a twofold task: (1) to throttle down the offense with the least possible amount of yardage, and (2) to prevent a touchdown (in the event that the first line of defense fails to do its job).

The defensive players are permitted to line up any way they want to, so long as all members of the defensive unit remain on their side of the line of scrimmage. Coaches have found, however, that the defense performs with its greatest efficiency when assignments are divided into these three areas of responsibility:

1. The front four—two ends and two tackles. Their job is to stifle attempts to run the ball and, in the case of a pass, to pressure the quarterback.

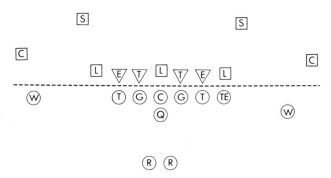

Offense faces defense across the line of scrimmage. Key to abbreviations, on offense: Q, quarterback; R, running backs; C, center; G, guards; T, tackles; TE, tight end; W, wide receivers; on defense: T, tackles; E, ends; L, linebackers; C, cornerbacks; S, safeties.

These men have to have good size but they also have to be very agile.

2. The secondary—the deep defensive backs, the two cornerbacks and two safeties. Their primary job is to cover prospective pass receivers, but they also must help out on running plays. Members of the secondary are the fastest players on the defensive unit.

3. The linebackers—men who have the physical capabilities of both the linemen and defensive backs—good size, strength, speed, and agility.

The usual pro football defense includes three linebackers—the middle linebacker and two outside linebackers, one on the right side, one on the left.

Sometimes they are called corner linebackers. The three men must work together as a cohesive unit.

The middle linebacker normally lines up opposite the offensive center. The outside linebackers adjust their positioning according to how the running backs and tight end line up. If the tight end stations himself toward the outside, the linebacker on that side (who may be referred to as the strong-side linebacker) moves a step or two toward the outside.

So much for tactics.

If the coach of your favorite team were to write out the specifications for the "perfect" linebacker, the description might read like this: run 40 yards in 4.8 or 4.9 seconds, 100 yards in 11 or 12 seconds; weight, 220–230 pounds; height, 6-foot-2 to 6-foot-4; quick reactions; good lateral pursuit, ability to run backward fast; intelligence; aggressiveness.

The statistics concerning height and weight don't have great meaning, however. Nick Buoniconti, for example, is 5-foot-10, 215 pounds. What he lacks in size he makes up for in quickness. Dave Robinson of the Redskins—6-foot-4, 245 pounds—is at the other extreme. But no one ever accused Robinson of being slow of foot. He was fast enough to be a pass receiver in college.

Another exception is Ted Hendricks of the Colts. He stands 6-foot-7. Trying to pass the ball over Hendricks is like trying to throw over the Empire State Building. So how tall a man is or how much he happens to weigh aren't crucial matters. What is

Nick Buoniconti of the Dolphins copes with several hundred pounds of blocking skill.

important is his ability to get the job done.

Two vital qualities are strength and quickness. When a running back comes careening out of the backfield, he is usually convoyed by a blocker or two. The linebacker has to be able to fight off the blocker, take hold of the ball carrier about the head and shoulders, and stop him cold. It takes real muscle power.

Quickness is just as important. Quickness is different from speed. Quickness is the ability to get moving before the opposition does, that is, a split second before the ball is snapped. George Allen, coach of the Redskins, calls it "instantaneous recognition and reaction."

This is what Dick Butkus of the Chicago Bears said about being quick: "You need a nose for the ball, an inkling as to where different things are going to come off. You have to be able to move laterally, and fight off the center on one side, and jump and dodge the tackle on the other side, and get out there and make the play on the end."

There is one other quality that linebackers must have and that is toughness. Indeed, in a sport that is often characterized by violence, linebackers are the most violent men of all. Ray Nitschke of the Packers once tackled a runner with such ferocity that the man was unconscious for ten minutes. George Webster of the Houston Oilers used to hit so hard that he was always bending his facemask out of shape.

Someone once wrote an article for a football magazine that was titled "The Science of Linebacking." That's a little bit laughable. There's about as much method and discipline to linebacking as there is to a painting by Jackson Pollock. Of course,

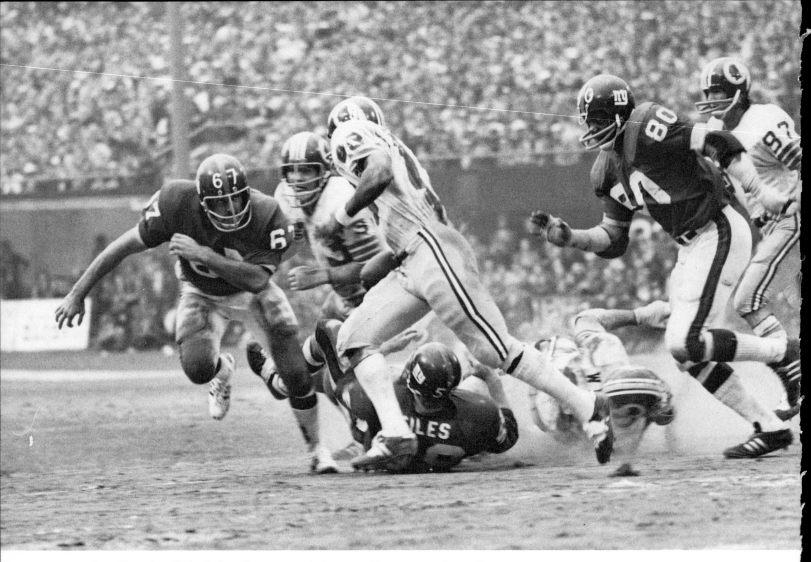

Ron Hornsby (67) of the Giants speeds into position to stop Larry Brown.

there are coaches who will tell you that linebacking is a science. There are also coaches who will tell you that hitting a blocking sled is a science, and they will draw you a hundred diagrams showing how it should be done.

What linebacking is, is hitting and tackling. It's a tough, hard-nosed business. Look at the linebacker's stance. His feet are spread, he's bent slightly at the waist. His fists are clenched. There are only a couple of other sports in which the ready position is like that of a linebacker's. One is boxing. Another is wrestling.

Super Crunch. King Kong. The Mad Stork. Killer. The Animal. The Head Hunter. These are the nicknames for some of pro football's linebackers. You get the idea that people with names like these don't make their living as accountants or schoolteachers.

A Dr. William J. Beausay, in a study recently completed, spent ten years in the psychological testing of NFL players. Quarterbacks he found to be "shy and self-disciplined." Running backs were "more outgoing, impulsive, and ego-driven." Linebackers he found to be "hostile, demanding, and retaliatory."

Willie Lanier would probably agree with these findings. He once summed up the business of linebacking in these words: "Trying to hurt somebody doesn't turn me on. Taking a swing at a guy at the sidelines isn't my bag.

13

Linebacking is hitting. Hitter is Chiefs' Willie Lanier.

"But I've always loved clean hitting. A good hit is beautiful. I enjoy it."

DEVELOPMENT OF THE ART

December 6, 1925, a sunny Sunday, rates as one of the most important dates in pro football history. The great Red Grange, the most electrifying player the game had ever produced, made his professional debut in New York City, leading the Chicago Bears into the Polo Grounds to face the Giants.

The outcome isn't what makes the game worth remembering (although the Giants managed to

Joe Alexander, on defense, a roving center.

win). The significant thing is the attendance. More than 65,000 fans jammed their way into the park to see Grange perform. It was pro football's first big gate and gave the game a sharp boost at a time it badly needed one.

In the days preceding the game, column after column of newspaper space was devoted to Grange and his Chicago teammates. The Giant players shrugged off the publicity. They believed they had the defenses to stop the Bears. The program for the game tipped off one aspect of New York's strategy. "He [Grange] must watch Joe Alexander, the husky center," warned the program. "He is a player calculated to smear Grange on many a play or at least ruin whatever interference has been prepared for him.

"Alexander has the reputation of following the ball closer than any other [player] in professional football, and any of the visiting teams will tell you that the way Alexander senses the direction of the play is truly uncanny."

If that description sounds something like that for a modern-day linebacker, it's no accident. What Joe Alexander and other centers of the 1920's did on defense was very similar to what Willie Lanier does today.

Most football historians say that the position of linebacker was invented in the early 1950's, when tactical changes were being introduced and the age of specialization was coming into full bloom. The

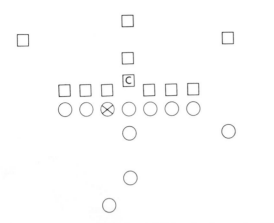

Only the "center on defense (C)" backed up the line in the 1920's.

first time the National Football League selected a trio of All-League linebackers was in 1952, which gave a kind of official status to the position.

Yet in pro football's earliest days, the 1920's, there were players who played the same role as linebackers do today. They charged forward to stop the run; they dropped off on passes. And they had the intelligence to figure out when to do which.

Pro football was quite different in the 1920's. One thing that made it different was that everyone played "both ways," on both offense and defense. Even the most noted players of the time were sixty-minute players.

Jim Thorpe, the first of the game's "name" players, is remembered as a pulverizing ball carrier,

able to grind enemy players into the ground, but he was also a savage tackler. He would hurl his body at an enemy runner, aiming at the man's legs. Sammy Baugh, the great passer of the 1930's, was also a defensive halfback, a cornerback in today's parlance.

So it was with Joe Alexander. When the Giants were on offense, Alexander was the center. Then when the opposition took over the ball, Joe dropped off to defend.

Many observers say that Alexander was the best of the early centers. An All-American at Syracuse, he began his pro career with the Rochester Jeffersons in 1921, played with the Milwaukee Badgers in 1922, and joined the Giants in 1925. He was head coach of the New York team in 1925 and 1926.

Sturdily built—5-foot-11, 220 pounds—and one of the few players of his time to wear a mustache, Alexander was not a plain, ordinary center, but a *roving* center, one of the first. In other words, he free-lanced.

The Giants of Alexander's time used a six-man line on defense. Alexander was stationed about two yards in back of the gap between guards, about where the middle linebacker is positioned today. But he was never called a linebacker. He was known simply as "the center of defense." So it was with other players; the fullback was "the fullback on defense."

On offense, teams of the 1920's and 1930's used

a single-wing formation. The quarterback's role was a minor one, usually as a blocker on running plays. The center snapped the ball back to the left halfback, or, as he was frequently called, the tailback.

The single wing, by getting a covey of blockers out in front of the ball carrier, put the stress on the running game. Besides having the quarterback and right halfback leading the way, the guards would pull from their positions in the line, then run laterally and get out in front of the ball carrier, too. Teams also passed the ball, but not very often.

"You were on your own when you played defense in those days," says Alexander, later a practicing physician in New York City. "Individual instinct and individual effort were what were important.

"When you saw a pass developing, you dropped back. When you saw an opening in the line, you'd plunge through it. No one called signals. No one told you what to do."

Alexander had exceptional quickness, and once on a place-kick attempt he shot through the line to take the ball right off the kicker's toe, then sprinted 80 yards for a touchdown. One season he scored three touchdowns on intercepted passes.

"We did all the things that modern linebackers do—blitzed, stunted, played zone defense and man-to-man," Alexander says. "But we didn't have name tags for everything the way they do today. You knew what you had to do and you did it."

During the late 1920's, teams began passing the

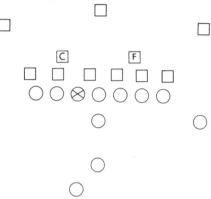

The 6-2-3 defense was used during the 1930's, with the center (C) and fullback (F) backing up.

ball more, certainly not with the frequency they do today, but at least more than they had been. The defense adjusted to this change by moving the fullback closer to the line to help out the center. This resulted in a 6-2-3 formation—a six-man front line, two men who backed up, and a three-man secondary. The 6-2-3 defense was used throughout most of the 1930's.

The outstanding backer-up of this period was a tall and solidly built All-American from Washington State University by the name of Mel Hein. One of the first "name" college players signed by the pros, Hein joined the New York Giants in 1931. His college coaches warned Hein of the evils of the pro game. "You'll be getting in with riffraff, with the wrong kind of people," he was told. "There'll be drinking and gambling and that kind of thing."

But Hein was planning on getting married and the lure of money—$150 a game—was too strong. He sat on the bench for the first few games, but when the Giants' regular center was injured, Hein went in as his replacement and was a regular from then on.

"We tried working on Hein," George Halas of the Chicago Bears once remarked, "but from the beginning he was too smart. We'd think he had overshifted and we'd try a play to the short side. Bang! Hein is there and he's pulling the man down. We'd try a short pass, thinking that he was going to rush, and he'd either bat it down or intercept. How he could get in your hair! Even as a rookie, there was no one else like him."

Hein, who later served as the NFL's assistant supervisor of officials, shrugs off such praise. "Linebacking wasn't as difficult then as it is nowadays," he says. "With the single wing, you could see play developing. You had an idea what was coming.

"When a running play went wide to my side, my job was to make sure that the ball carrier didn't get outside of me. On passes, we played man-to-man. I picked up the first receiver who swung out of the backfield."

The year 1938 was Hein's best. The Giants won the Eastern Division crown and faced the Packers, champions in the West, for the NFL crown. More than 48,000 fans paid their way into New York's

Mel Hein

Polo Grounds to watch, a record crowd for a title match.

During the first quarter, the Packer offense targeted on Hein, aiming play after play at his position. That was no surprise. What was surprising was that Green Bay was able to march steadily down the field. Alarmed at what was happening, New York coach Steve Owen called Hein to the sidelines.

"What's going on out there?" Owen asked.

"Don't worry," said Hein. "I'm giving them the short yardage." And then he explained that his greatest concern was to blunt the Green Bay passing attack, Arnie Herber throwing to the great Don Hutson.

Hein's strategy paid dividends. New York led at the end of the half, 16-14. But Hein had been kicked in the head and suffered a concussion. He couldn't remember where he was. He couldn't even remember his name.

With Hein on the sidelines, the Packers stormed back, taking the second-half kickoff all the way to the New York 15-yard line. They then booted a field goal to move out in front, 17-16. Before the quarter ended, however, the Giants were in command again, 23-17.

That's the way it stood in the game's closing minutes. The Packers had possession and prepared to launch their last offensive drive. The crowd roared as Hein trotted out onto the field, his head still throbbing as if there were a hundred hammers pounding inside it. The New York defenders dug in and the Green Bay attack fizzled. The gun sounded. The Giants were the champions. Hein was later named the NFL's Player of the Year.

"You had to be in good condition to play sixty minutes," Hein recalls. "Remember, we were in for all the kickoffs and punts and so we did plenty of running, and this helped to keep us in condition.

"Of course, when you played sixty minutes you paced yourself. You didn't play the fourth quarter with quite the same enthusiasm that you played the first. Both teams began slowing down as the game progressed.

"And you didn't go all out on every play. If you were playing defensive end and the opposition ran a sweep around the other end, you weren't likely to pursue the ball carrier. You'd stand and watch.

"The tempo of the game is entirely different today. It's much, much faster. Not only are the players capable of greater speed, but they're encouraged to run full-tilt on every down."

The Giants feted Hein with a "day" in 1940 to salute his decade of excellence. He was awarded silverware, luggage, and an automobile. The Giants played the Brooklyn Dodgers that afternoon and lost, 14-6. But it wasn't Hein's fault. "Hein was a heroic figure in the New York cause," said a newspaper account of the game, "the only defender who tackled with authority."

Hein was chosen an All-Pro center no less than eight times. He was named a charter member of Pro Football's Hall of Fame, also as a center. But it is as a backer-up that Hein likes to be remembered.

"That's how I made my name—backing up the line," he says. "And I made it bumping into some

MEL HEIN—HIS DAY

N. Y. Giants vs. Brooklyn Dodgers

CAPTAIN MEL HEIN
The Giants' All-Time Center

POLO GROUNDS   **Sunday, Dec. 1, 1940**

pretty tough people. Besides, who ever remembers an offensive center?"

About midway in Hein's career—he retired in 1945—pro football went through another period of tactical change when teams began discarding the single wing in favor of the T-formation. In the T, the quarterback positions himself directly in back of the center and handles the ball on every play. He can then hand the ball to another back, run with it himself, or throw a forward pass. And whatever he planned to do, he could conceal his intent until the last instant.

On December 8, 1940, the Chicago Bears destroyed the Washington Redskins in the NFL championship game by a score of 73-0, and they used the T-formation in wreaking their destruction. After that, the swing to the T was on.

"The T places tremendous pressure on the backers-up," Steve Owen, coach of the Giants, observed in 1943. "They must hold their moves momentarily to diagnose fakes and wait for the play to develop. The backers-up get no second guess. When they're fooled, the T moves."

In an effort to cope with the T, coaches began using a 5-3-3 defense. Three men, not merely two, are assigned to back up the line.

The New York Giants used the 5-3-3 as early as 1933 in a game against the Bears, according to Mel Hein. "But," says Hein, "it didn't work well. The linebackers weren't agile enough. Steve Owen, the

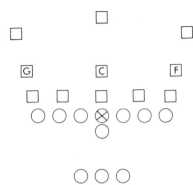

When the T-formation was introduced, the defense answered with the 5-3-3, three men backing up, the fullback (F), a guard (G), and the center (C).

Giant coach, quickly dropped it." Not until the late 1930's did the Giants and other teams begin using the 5-3-3 consistently.

Sometimes the Giants would blitz from the 5-3-3. "We didn't call it blitzing," Mel Hein recalls. "We called it stunting. When we wanted to rush in to get the passer, I'd call a right-side stunt, a left-side stunt, or a middle stunt. If it was a right-side stunt, I'd be the one to go in, and the tackle and end on my side would cover the area I'd vacated.

"We also had a middle stunt, in which everyone went in—the fullback, the middle guard, and me."

While Mel Hein was the outstanding backer-up of the 1930's, Clyde (Bulldog) Turner of the Chicago Bears was the dominant figure in the position during the 1940's. In his thirteen-year career, which

began in 1940, Turner was an All-League choice six times, and he helped the Bears win four NFL championships.

Turner, like Mel Hein, is a member of Pro Football's Hall of Fame. Also like Hein, Turner was

The Bears' Bulldog Turner

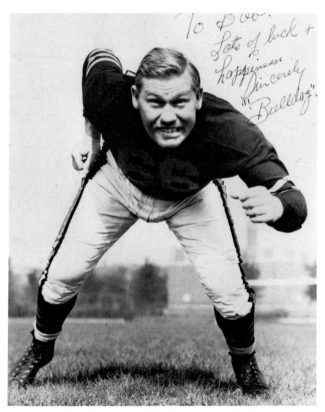

Ted Fritsch of the Packers (right) tries to figure out a way to get around Bulldog Turner.

primarily a center, and backing up the line was what he did on defense. He was built like a center, stocky and muscular.

On defense, the Bears used both the 6-2-2-1 and 5-3-2-1 alignments, switching from one to the other. The position Turner played would be comparable to that of right linebacker today.

"In my time," Turner once recalled, "we had a lot harder job on pass coverage than linebackers nowadays. We had to cover fast halfbacks man-to-man, which made us about comparable to today's cornerbacks or safeties."

Despite his bulk, Turner had surprising quickness, and was considered one of the fastest linemen in pro football. Coach George Halas of the Bears wanted Turner to maintain his reputation, and threatened to fine him $50 if he ever permitted his weight to get above 232 pounds. Since Turner's bonus for signing with the Bears amounted to $150, and his salary as a rookie was not much above $2,000, he watched his weight very carefully.

Turner was a wizard at intercepting passes. He led the league in 1942 with eight steals, a mark no other linebacker has ever equalled. The interception that was Turner's greatest thrill came in 1947. The Bears faced the Redskins. It was Washington's ball on the Chicago 4-yard line.

The Redskins' great passer, Sammy Baugh, darted back and threw. Turner made the interception and started running. He cut one way and then the other, sidestepping tacklers, changing speed, and using his blockers like an accomplished running back. As he crossed the Washington 10-yard line, Baugh sprinted up from behind and leaped on Turner's shoulders. Turner never even slowed down, carrying Baugh across the goal line. He had run 96 yards.

Teams of the late 1940's and early 1950's learned to attack the 5-3-3 defense with passes. The Los Angeles Rams would send four and five receivers into a pattern, some men short and others long. The Cleveland Browns, spreading the ends wide, specialized in sideline passes, with the deadly accurate Otto Graham to do the throwing.

The Browns captured the championship of the All-America Football Conference in each of the four years of its existence, and when, in 1950, the AAFC folded and the Browns switched to the NFL, they continued their winning ways. Steve Owen of the New York Giants devised a defense to throttle down the Cleveland attack. He called it an umbrella defense, because the way in which the backs were aligned resembled an open umbrella. It was also known as the 6-1-4 defense.

The first time that the Giants met the Browns the

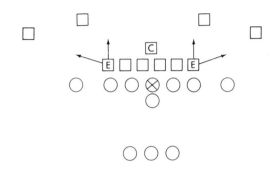

When the Cleveland Browns spread their receivers, the New York Giants came up with the 6-1-4, the umbrella defense. The ends (E) either rushed or dropped back.

umbrella worked perfectly. Sometimes the ends rushed; other times they dropped back to help out on pass coverage. New York halted Otto Graham without a completion during the first half and were able to shut out the Browns, something that had never happened before in pro football history.

One of Owen's defensive backs that afternoon was a tall, slim, and balding player, a sure-armed tackler who seldom took gambles. His name was Tom Landry. When Steve Owen retired and Landry took over as the Giants' defensive coach in 1954, he made another change, pulling the ends off the line. In other words, the 6-1-4 became the 4-3-4.

The 4-3-4 was pro football's basic defense during the 1960's and into the 1970's. But it wasn't Landry's only contribution. He instructed his defensive

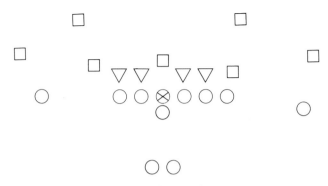

The 6-1-4 led directly to the modern 4-3-4.

players to read "keys," to check the way the opposition was aligned and prepare to react accordingly. "Now what did the coach say to do against this formation?" a player would ask himself. "What is my key? What is my responsibility?" Landry has since added lustre to his name as head coach of the Dallas Cowboys.

Something else was happening at this time, and it was to have as much significance in the development of the defensive game as the switch from the single wing to the T or the introduction of the umbrella. Pro football was becoming specialized, very specialized.

The era of specialization had its beginnings during World War II. Players were being called into the service and a talent shortage developed. The NFL reacted by adopting a free-substitution rule, which enabled a coach to send a man in from the bench just about whenever he wanted to. The free-substitution rule was adopted permanently in 1950.

The rule meant that kickers could concentrate on either place-kicking or punting, whichever their specialty happened to be. It meant that quarterbacks could devote all of their time and effort to becoming better passers and strategists. As for the men who backed up the line—linebackers, as they were now being called—they no longer had to be concerned with centering the ball, playing fullback, or any other offensive responsibilities.

The first player to win national prominence solely for his skills as a linebacker was Sam Huff of the New York Giants. Scrappy and hard-nosed, Huff joined the Giants in 1956, following a well-regarded career at West Virginia.

Huff not only benefited from the game's tactical changes and the fact that he never had to play on offense, but his career was also aided by the media. "The Violent World of Sam Huff" was the title of a half-hour television documentary that gave millions of viewers a realistic glimpse of what it was like to play middle linebacker. A microphone was placed in Sam's helmet and those tuning in could hear the loud whack of colliding bodies and the resulting grunts and gasps for air.

Sam appeared on the cover of *Time* magazine and he endorsed more products than all the quarterbacks of the day combined. This was a period when the Giants and Browns were deadly rivals, and Sam's

Sam Huff

Sunday duels with Jimmy Brown, Cleveland's great running back, received in-depth coverage. So popular was he with fans at Yankee Stadium that they would chant "Huff-Huff-Huff-Huff-Huff" whenever he made a decisive tackle.

Once, in a game against the San Francisco 49ers, Huff made one of his most memorable tackles. San Francisco quarterback Y. A. Tittle called a screen pass, then looped the ball to fullback Hugh McElhenny, who had two big linemen, Lou Palatella and Bruce Bosley, out in front of him. Huff read the play perfectly, and even before Tittle had sent the ball on its way, he was thundering toward McElhenny. He plunged his left fist into Bosley's chest and his right into Palatella's, sending the two men sprawling backward into McElhenny for a loss on the play.

Huff, at 6-foot-1, 220 pounds, wasn't particularly big. He was never noted for his speed. But he was a scrapper. "You've got to be mean," he once said. "The minute I come out for a game, I say to myself, 'I'm going to be the meanest guy on the field. I'm going to give it to anyone I can get a shot at. Look out for ol' Sam. He's mean today.'"

Huff displayed his meanness for the Giants for eight years, and in six of those the team won the conference championship, and they won the NFL crown once. After Huff was traded to the Redskins in 1963, the Giants went into a sudden decline. Most Giant rooters say it was more than a coincidence.

There were other linebackers of the 1950's who were Huff's equal in terms of skill and dedication. They just didn't happen to earn as many headlines as Sam did.

One was Chuck Bednarik. Bednarik toiled for the Philadelphia Eagles, winning All-Pro honors eight times. His rookie year was 1949, a season in which the Eagles won the NFL championship. But after that, one losing season piled on another. Indeed, Bednarik had to wait eleven years before the Eagles were poised to win the title again. In December, 1960, Philadelphia, having won the Eastern Conference championship, faced the Green Bay Packers for the NFL crown.

Play was in the fourth quarter, the Eagles leading, 17-13. Quarterback Bart Starr had the Packers on the march. A Starr pass was good for a 20-yard gain and a first down on the Philadelphia 30-yard line. Starr darted back again. This time he connected with Gary Knafelc for an eight-yard gain.

There was less than a minute remaining and the clock was running. The Packers didn't even bother to huddle.

"Cover the end!" Bednarik yelled to the deep men. "Cover for the pass!"

A pass was just what Starr had in mind. He pedaled back quickly, searching for a receiver. When he saw they were covered, he had no choice but to loop the ball to fullback Jimmy Taylor.

Taylor made the catch, put his head down, and charged for the end zone. At the 10-yard line, Eagle

Chuck Bednarik

25

safety Don Burroughs made a leap for Taylor and missed. Linebacker Maxie Baughan got his arms around Taylor's waist, but Taylor churned free. Now Bednarik closed in. "I saw our guys hitting him and bouncing off," Bednarik was to say later, "so I told myself, 'I'm not bouncing off.'"

Bednarik went in high, wrapping his powerful arms around Taylor's shoulders, and then he squeezed, the arms closing like a steel collar. Taylor crumpled to the ground.

The whistle blew to end the play. But Bednarik, lying on top of the fallen Green Bay fullback, wouldn't release him from his iron grip. The clock was still running and Bednarik knew it. As the final gun sounded, Bednarik's face broke into a wide grin. "OK, Jimmy," he said, "you can get up now."

Bednarik was a throwback, for during most of his career he was a sixty-minute man, playing offensive

Eagles celebrate in their dressing room following their victory in the 1960 NFL championship. Left to right: Bill Barnes, Chuck Bednarik, coach Buck Shaw, Norm Van Brocklin, and Ted Dean.

center as well as linebacker. Philadelphia coach Buck Shaw singled him out for special praise after the Eagles had won the league championship in 1960. "We've got to thank the old pro," Shaw declared, "and I mean Bednarik. He held us together on defense—and offense."

Eagle quarterback Norm Van Brocklin had his own words of tribute. "If Chuck had played for the New York Giants," he said, "they would be erecting a statue of him under the flagpole at Yankee Stadium." No one had to ask Van Brocklin who he was making reference to.

While fans of the New York Giants were loyal to Sam Huff, and Philadelphians supported Chuck Bednarik who, incidentally, was named to the Hall of Fame in 1969, most football experts single out Joe Schmidt of the Detroit Lions as the best linebacker in the business in the period from the mid-1950's to the early 1960's. Schmidt was an All-Pro selection in eight of the thirteen seasons he played and he was named his team's Most Valuable Player four times.

Schmidt had an instinct for where the ball was going to go. Lou Creekmur, one of his teammates, once remarked that Schmidt had "a football sense that comes once in a lifetime." Creekmur said that Schmidt could "smell the ball." Another teammate, Gene Gedman, put it this way: "Joe has a little something extra, a sixth sense, extrasensory perception—something."

Schmidt was often referred to as a "mean but clean tackler," a description that he would probably agree with. "A good hard tackle gives you a lift, a thrill," he once said. "I don't mean to sound sadistic, but I enjoy tackling."

Schmidt's method of tackling was to hit low. "In a situation where the back has two or three steps on you and is coming at full speed, if you don't get low he'll run over you. I try to hit him in the thighs, the knees, as low as I can."

Joseph Paul Schmidt was his full name. He was born in Pittsburgh in 1932, and learned his football on the sandlots of western Pennsylvania, playing on a team coached by his older brother. He was a fullback in high school, and talented enough to win a scholarship to the University of Pittsburgh. There he was converted to a linebacker by coach Len Casanova. He won some All-America recognition during his senior year, but injuries hampered him. Joe hoped to be drafted by the Steelers, but the Pittsburgh team was unwilling to take a chance on him because of his injury record. He was picked by the Lions in the seventh round.

Detroit had just won the NFL title and had talent at every position. Joe felt he didn't have the slightest chance of making the team. "Give it a try," his brother advised him. "What have you got to lose?"

Not a big man—5-foot-11, 215 pounds—Schmidt was awed by the size of the Detroit players. "What am I doing here?" he asked himself at training camp.

27

Joe Schmidt crunches a Colt ball carrier to the ground.

But in his first scrimmage Schmidt showed he was a fierce and canny defender. He intercepted three of Bobby Layne's passes and hammered hard at the veteran players. In one scrimmage he hit veteran guard Vince Banonis with such ferocity that Banonis could hardly pick himself up after the play. Schmidt was sure he was in for a tongue lashing, but all Banonis said was, "That's the way to hit, kid."

Banonis wasn't the only one that Schmidt impressed. Detroit coaches gave approving nods to the way he hit people. But winning acceptance from his teammates was much more difficult. In those days, the Lions, like many pro teams, treated rookies like outcasts. "No one talked to me at training camp," Schmidt once recalled. "Not even the other rookies."

Quarterback Bobby Layne reigned like a feudal monarch. The rookies would be awakened at 2:00 or 3:00 A.M. to go out and buy food, usually pizza, for Layne. Or they'd be made to serve Layne breakfast in bed.

Not long before the season opened, the Lions traded away veteran linebacker Dick Flanagan. While Schmidt didn't realize it at the time, this was an indication that he had made the team. The trade was upsetting to the other veteran players. At the Lions' annual preseason dinner, Bobby Layne walked over to where Schmidt was sitting. "You're the guy who's going to be taking Flanagan's place," he said. "I've got one piece of advice for you. You'd better do the job." Then he turned and walked away.

Schmidt continued to get the silent treatment from the veteran players until almost midseason. Then one day after a game he was invited out to Jimmy Kelly's, a local nightclub much favored by Layne and his followers. When Schmidt walked into Kelly's, Layne, serving as an impromptu master of ceremonies, demanded that he get up on the stage and sing a song. It was then that he knew he finally "belonged." "I began to enjoy being a part of pro football," he recalls.

Schmidt had a fine season in 1956, but 1957 was exceptional. The Lions, driving for the championship of the Western Conference, faced the Cleveland Browns in a crucial contest. As the game entered its final minutes, the Lions clung to a 10-7 lead. It was Cleveland's ball. Again and again quarterback Milt Plum sent Jimmy Brown hurtling into the line, and each time Schmidt would slam into Brown and stop him cold. The Lions hung on to win.

Detroit ended the season in a tie with the San Francisco 49ers for the Western Conference championship, necessitating a play-off. Y. A. Tittle, the 49ers' premiere passer, was having one of his best seasons, and he got the team off to a fast start, throwing for three touchdowns before the Lions even got on the scoreboard. At half time, San Francisco led, 24-7.

The third period began on much the same note for Detroit. On the very first play from scrimmage, Hugh McElhenny, San Francisco's star running back, broke into the open and sprinted 71 yards to the Detroit 9-yard line before he was dragged out of bounds.

Schmidt was furious. "It's too damn bad I've got to play with yellow quitters!" he screamed, stalking up and down in back of his linemen. "What a crummy bunch of doggers this is!" The Detroit defense got tough. San Francisco was unable to move the ball.

Their defensive stand gave the Lions fresh hope. When the offense took over, quarterback Tobin Rote quickly marched the team to a touchdown.

On the sidelines, meanwhile, Buster Ramsey, the Lions' defensive coach, instructed Schmidt to begin blitzing. The result was that quarterback Tittle spent much of the rest of the afternoon on his back looking at the sky, and when he did happen to get a chance to throw, he was usually off balance or had to hurry. The game turned out to be a disaster for him. The Lions came back to win, 31-27. "I got to Tittle quite a bit," Schmidt conceded afterward, fighting back a grin.

The Lions were easy winners in the NFL title game. Schmidt had a splendid day. As the gun sounded ending the game, Detroit fans streamed out onto the field. Instead of heading for the quarterback or coach, they converged upon Schmidt, hoist-

Schmidt had trying moments as the Lions' coach.

ing him to their shoulders and parading him around the field.

In the years that followed, the Lions were acknowledged to have the most fearsome defense in pro football and Schmidt was its hub. "He's a great tackler and strong leader," coach Vince Lombardi of the Green Bay Packers said of him, "and he can diagnose plays in an instant."

Schmidt retired as a player in 1965, and two years later he became the Lions' coach, a post he held for five years. Although the team once earned a play-off berth during his tenure, they failed to win a single championship. Once, in an attempt to explain the frustrations he experienced as a coach, Schmidt said, "I expect everyone to like me. I guess," he added, "that's a mistake."

No book having to do with linebacking would be complete without mentioning a frequent opponent of Joe Schmidt, Ray Nitschke of the Green Bay Packers. Nitschke first signed with the Packers in 1957 and stayed on for fifteen years. In 1969, when the NFL was celebrating its fiftieth anniversary, Nitschke was named the league's "All 50-Year Middle Linebacker." It will be the year 2019 before anyone can get that kind of recognition again.

Nitschke, fiery, bald, and toothless, was a football ruffian, the first linebacker known chiefly for his toughness. "He was the kind of guy," Dick Butkus once observed, "who would take on the blocker and really label him." (To Butkus, the word "label"

Ray Nitschke

is a synonym for clobber or bash.) "The linebacker isn't supposed to be blocked," Butkus continued, "so I avoid being blocked. I try to get there any way I can without being hit, without being contained. Not Nitschke. He'll punish the blocker on the way to get the ball carrier."

Nitschke went all-out in every game he ever played. He even went full-tilt in Packer practice sessions. In 1962, the Packers were preparing to play the New York Giants for the NFL championship. Lombardi, dissatisfied with the way the practice session was going, yelled at his defensive unit, "Hit those guys like they're Giants!"

That was all that Nitschke needed to hear. On the very next play, he slammed into center Jimmy Ringo so ferociously that Ringo suffered a pinched nerve in his neck, and for a time it was feared he would miss the game. "I couldn't see Ringo there at all," Nitschke explained after. "To me, he was Ray Wietecha, the Giant center. That's why I busted him."

Born in Elmwood Park, Illinois, in 1936, Nitschke's boyhood was touched with tragedy. His father was killed in a streetcar accident when he was three, and his mother died when he was a high-school freshman, leaving him to be raised by an older brother.

"He was good to me," Nitschke once recalled, "but I never had any discipline. I grew up belting the other kids in the neighborhood. I felt I was somebody who didn't have anything, so I took it out on other people."

As a senior at Proviso High School in nearby Maywood, Ray played quarterback and safety. "He fought for every yard on offense," his coach said, "and was the meanest kid we had on defense. I remember how he threw an elbow at a guy coming downfield and we got fifteen yards for roughing. You don't see that happen to a safety very often."

Nitschke received a scholarship to the University of Illinois, where he played fullback and linebacker. As a Packer rookie, Nitschke broke into the lineup frequently, but only because the No. 1 middle linebacker was sidelined with injuries. It wasn't until Vince Lombardi took over at Green Bay that Nitschke began to fulfill his potential. There was never any question about his toughness or ability to hit. Lombardi made him a finished player by stressing the importance of reading keys and analyzing opposition strategy.

Nitschke has high praise for Lombardi and the way in which the late Packer coach influenced him. "I learned things from him that will stay with me the rest of my life," says Nitschke. "He was hard, a disciplinarian, but I believe he really loved us all. I know he made me the player I became." Nitschke says that he enjoyed "every game, every moment" during the Lombardi years.

Under Lombardi and with Nitschke, the Packers won five NFL championships and the first two

The violent tackle was the usual thing for Ray Nitschke.

Super Bowls as well. When Green Bay played Oakland in Super Bowl II, Nitschke was the man the Raiders feared the most. Ray showed that their fears were not misplaced by making nine tackles.

Through most of the 1960's, Nitschke reigned as the No. 1 middle linebacker in pro football. In 1968, *Sport* Magazine polled five former great linebackers in an effort to establish "The Best Middle Linebacker in Pro Football." Nitschke was the majority choice. Joe Schmidt, in explaining why his vote went to Nitschke, said, "He is particularly quick. . . . He has amazing lateral quickness and mobility, and that is of prime importance to the middle linebacker."

Bill Pellington, a standout linebacker with the Colts for many seasons, praised Nitschke not only for his skills but his leadership qualities. "He's the core of the team," said Pellington. "He's able to direct it, he's such an inspiring type of guy. He's a real hustler, a talker. He always puts out."

In the final seasons of his career, Nitschke was often relegated to the bench, yet he still maintained his enthusiasm for the game. How did he feel about watching from the sidelines? "I can't complain about whatever the Packers do," he said. "They've always been fair to me. . . . But it hurts not to start. I have a lot of pride."

Once, toward the end of his career, a reporter asked Nitschke what game of the nearly two hundred he had played stood out in his memory.

Nitschke answered without hesitation. "The NFL championship in 1962."

The Giants were the Packers' opponents. The game was played at Yankee Stadium in New York on a bitter cold day. The field was patched with ice and throughout the afternoon a wicked wind whipped the players. In the first quarter, Nitschke blitzed in to deflect one of Y. A. Tittle's passes, and the ball ended up in the hands of Dan Currie, the Packers' left linebacker, ending a New York drive. In the second quarter, Nitschke recovered a fumble that led to a Green Bay touchdown, and he recovered a second fumble in the third quarter to set up a field goal. The Packers took the game, 16-7.

After the game, Nitschke slumped on a bench in front of his locker stall. His body was a mass of welts and bruises. Blood trickled from his forehead. His hands were swollen, the fingers raw and bleeding. Because of the frozen ground, he hadn't been able to move with his usual agility and he was disappointed with his performance. Others disagreed. While Nitschke was sitting there pulling the tape from his knuckles, he was brought the news that he had been voted the game's Most Valuable Player.

Nitschke remained a favorite of the Packers right up until 1973, the year that he retired. Whenever No. 66 trotted out onto the field, he was greeted with a standing ovation, even at some road games.

Nitschke's retirement represented the end of an era. Nitschke, Joe Schmidt, and Chuck Bednarik had demonstrated how the position of linebacker was to be played. They set the standards. And they, along with Sam Huff, established the mystique of the position. Those who were to come—Dick Butkus, Tommy Nobis, Willie Lanier, Mike Curtis, and the others—had a solid foundation upon which to build.

Pro football is somewhat more sophisticated today than it was during the years that Joe Schmidt and Ray Nitschke were seeking to establish their eminence. For one thing, many variations of the basic 4-3 defense are being used. One of the most noted is the "stack," which refers to a formation in which one or more of the linebackers plays directly behind defensive linemen. Stacking helps conceal the linebackers from the offensive players and, thus,

Stacked defense conceals a linebacker (L) behind a tackle.

they are less likely to be blocked out of a play. It also gives the linebackers more tackling room.

In Super Bowl IV, Kansas City vs. Minnesota, the Chiefs stacked two and sometimes three of their linebackers. The concept was new to the Vikings and quarterback Joe Kapp found it difficult to cope with, a significant factor in the Chiefs' victory.

What about defensive formations of the future? What are they going to be like? What took place in Super Bowl VII, in which the Miami Dolphins whipped the Washington Redskins, gives a clue. Both teams employed "situation substituting" on defense, that is, they varied the types of players they used—especially linebackers and linemen—depending on the down-and-distance situation.

The Dolphins used what they call a "5-3 defense" (named for linebacker Bob Matheson's uniform number). Matheson was put in as a fourth linebacker, replacing a lineman. Depending on the situation, he lined up as a linebacker or defensive end.

The Redskins on defense moved a linebacker into the line when they expected a run, giving them a 5-2-4 alignment. They went to the more conventional 4-3-4 on second and third downs when medium yardage was needed and substituted a fifth defensive back for a linebacker in obvious passing situations, an alignment they referred to as their "nickel defense."

Bob Matheson, No. 53

Obviously, then, the game is becoming more and more specialized. In the years just ahead, a team may have some linebackers whose specialty is stopping running plays, and others whose skills are best suited toward preventing pass receptions. They will be switched in and out of the lineup as the game changes.

There also has been talk in recent years of using a three-man line and switching from three linebackers to four of them. It's said that such a system would make blocking assignments more confusing for the offense and, at the same time, give a team improved defensive coverage, especially on passes.

Quarterbacks, running backs, and other offensive-team personnel are not likely to be in favor of such a change. Three linebackers, they realize, are plenty; four of them could be embarrassing.

TACTICS AND STRATEGY

Chuck Bednarik, who was named to the Hall of Fame on the basis of his stormy career as a linebacker for the Eagles, was once asked what the difference was between a middle linebacker and an outside, or corner, linebacker. "That's easy," said Bednarik. "The corner linebacker plays golf on Tuesday, but not the middle linebacker. He can't lift his arms until the end of the week."

Obviously, this is an exaggeration. Yet it is conceded, even by men who play the outside, that the man in the middle has the toughest job. It's like being a cop at a very busy intersection; something's always happening.

The corner linebackers are very busy, too. Actually, the biggest difference between the outside linebackers and the middle linebacker is not in how they play but in *where* they play.

The middle linebacker has to serve as a link between the linemen and the secondary, and as such he must have some of the qualities or each—the size of a lineman, or close to it, and nearly the speed of a deep man.

He is much more a part of the line than the outside men. Everything he does has to be coordinated with the men in the line, which is one reason that he calls defensive formations. Some experts say that it's an advantage for the middle linebacker to have had experience as a defensive lineman. Bobby

Bell of the Kansas City Chiefs was a college tackle at Minnesota. Tommy Nobis of the Atlanta Falcons was a guard at the University of Texas. There are many other examples.

The middle man is almost always bigger than the other two because he has to be able to handle blocks thrown by the center and guards, men who are likely to weigh 250-260 pounds, maybe even more. There are exceptions, of course. Joe Schmidt, who won All-NFL honors eight times as middle linebacker for the Detroit Lions, was 6-foot-1, 215 pounds. But Schmidt had a pair of giant tackles in front of him—Alex Karras at 250 pounds and Roger Brown at very close to 300.

Mobility is a "must" characteristic for each of the outside linebackers, because each has a big area to cover. They have to be able to stop runs to the inside and force wide plays back toward the middle. On slants and dive plays, the outside man covers from the center of the field to the sideline, alert for screen passes, look-ins and short hooks. Sometimes the outside linebacker has to cover a back on a man-to-man basis, which means he will be ranging 20 to 25 yards downfield.

There is a difference between playing on the right side and playing on the left. The linebacker who lines up on the left (to the left of the middle linebacker) usually has to contend with the tight end. He's known as the strong-side linebacker.

Covering the tight end is no easy task. Most of

Agility is a must. Redskin linebackers practice footwork, forward and back.

them are big men, 235 to 240 pounds, and they are about the strongest players in the game. The linebacker who's assigned to tight end must take the initiative. He can't wait for the man to make his move; he has to beat him.

As the ball is snapped, the linebacker takes a step forward and slams the tight end with a forearm. If the tight end's mission is to block, the blow is meant to put him at a disadvantage. If he's planning to go out for a pass, he's slowed down. After the initial "pop," the tight end usually becomes the responsibility of the safety on that side of the field, and the linebacker has a new worry, a running back who may be circling out of the backfield as a pass receiver.

Most teams like to send their running plays to the tight end's side, which means that the strong-side linebacker sometimes sees as much action as the man in the middle.

The weak-side linebacker, because he does not have to worry about the tight end, is more of a free spirit, going wherever the ball goes. When instructing fans in how to watch a football game, some experts advise watching the weak-side linebacker as a tip-off as to where the play is going to go. "He always goes where the ball goes," it's said.

The weak-side linebacker's principal enemies are the wide receiver and pulling guards. These are the men most frequently assigned to block him.

Some teams flip-flop their outside linebackers, depending on how the offense lines up. When Chuck Howley was a member of the Dallas Cowboys' linebacking crew, he was known for his fluid, free-wheeling style. Dave Edwards, the other outside linebacker, was stronger than Howley and better at fighting off the tight end's block. So Edwards always lined up on the tight end's side, the strong side. Howley always took the weak side.

When the ball is snapped, the linebackers must go forward, back, or race laterally. There's little that can be done right behind the line. Each must move, driving in to plug a hole or dropping off to protect against a pass. For the men who coach linebackers, the slogan could be, "Don't stand there, do something!"

The linebacker's stance has to enable him to move quickly in any direction, which means it has to be what the "how-to" books call a two-point stance. The man is upright, evenly balanced, his knees flexed, and he bends slightly at the waist. Another reason for staying upright is that it permits the linebacker to see what's happening across the line in the offensive backfield.

Some coaches want their linebackers to position their feet in a particular way, the left foot forward if the man is stationed on the left side, for example. But this really isn't important. What is important is that the man be able to move quickly in any direction.

Linebackers—the middle linebacker, in particular—are often instructed to stunt before the ball is snapped, to jump in and out of the line of scrimmage in frantic fashion as the quarterback calls signals, sometimes filling a gap, at other times exchanging positions with a tackle or end. It gives the quarterback and the offensive team, in general, something else to think about.

During a game, if you watch the linebackers care-

Kansas City's Bob Stein (66) is ready to move in any direction.

fully, you will notice that they often seem to have an instinctive talent for going where the ball goes. They diagnose the play so quickly it's as if they listened in on the offensive team's huddle. This is because they are skilled in "keying" on, or "reading," the opposition players. They are able to detect certain mannerisms that tip off the play.

Although no two linebackers key in exactly the same way, certain generalities apply. The middle linebacker usually checks the set position of the running backs before anything else. One particular alignment may indicate a running play the team favors; another may tip off that they're sending a back out for a pass. Next, the middle linebacker notes how the receivers, the tight end included, are lined up. Third, he checks the spacing between

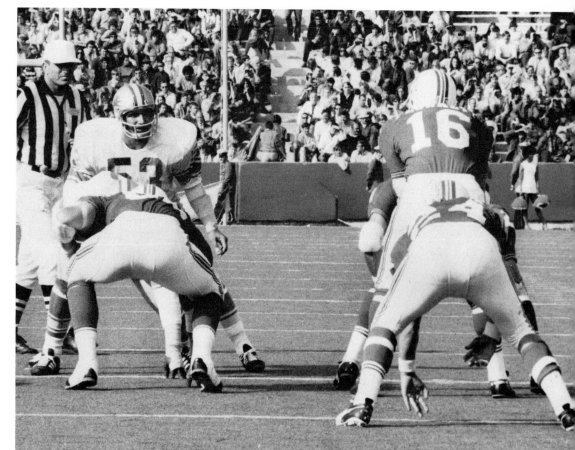

Mike Lucci concentrates—keys—as Jim Plunkett (16) calls signals.

players in the offensive line. Since he's three or four steps back, he has a better idea of the "splits," as they are called, than his own linemen. If he sees that the spacing is such that one of his own men is overburdened, he will change the spacing in his team's line.

Dick Butkus read quarterbacks by watching their feet as they got into position behind the center. Each man had his own eccentricities as he got set, Butkus found. If the quarterback's left foot was back, he was likely to be rolling to the left side. If his right foot was back, it probably meant he was going to drop straight back. "Some of them even drop back differently, depending on which way they're going to throw the ball," said Butkus in his book, *Stop Action*. "It just takes experience and a quarterback who doesn't study his own moves on the game films."

Butkus also sought to gather intelligence by peering into the huddle and trying to watch the quarterback's lips and read what he's saying. Sometimes you don't even have to have lip-reading skill. Joe Kapp, quarterback for the Vikings during the late 1960's, used to call out his plays in the huddle in such a loud voice that Butkus says he overheard him 80 per cent of the time.

As the game unfolds, the middle linebacker keeps adding to his store of information and refining his keys. Maybe he comes to the realization that the offense is directing its ground attack at an injured or inexperienced player, or perhaps passes are be-ing targeted on a particular weakness in the secondary. If so, the linebacker can revise the coverage so that the man under pressure gets help.

Once the ball is snapped, many other keys develop. The guards give several clues. They will block straight ahead, to the right or left, or if a pass is coming, they will stand erect, elbows at their chest, to protect the quarterback. Or the guards may pull, step back, and then run laterally to lead a running back as he attempts to sweep an end. A pulling guard can also indicate a trap block, a block on a defensive man who has been allowed to cross the line of scrimmage.

When a guard pulls and heads to the right, the linebacker usually takes it to mean that the play is going to the right side, so he heads in that direction. If the guard blocks straight ahead so as to open a hole, the linebacker fires ahead to plug it. If the guard sets up to pass block, the linebacker drops back into the secondary, watching the receivers and the quarterback as he goes.

Experienced linebackers learn to read keys that are very subtle. Maybe a lineman adjusts his hands or feet in such a way that he indicates the direction in which he is going to block. Or perhaps a lineman or a back leans in a particular direction before the ball is snapped. Sometimes a linebacker can read the amount of pressure a lineman is putting on his knuckles, and know whether the man is going to drop back and pass block or fire ahead.

The outside linebackers have four or five keys on each play, and they read them off in rapid succession. The strong-side linebacker keys on the tight end first. If the man tries to get free for a pass, the linebacker must slam into him, drive him to the ground, do something to stop him. Or the tight end may try to block the linebacker, in which case he has to fight him off.

His second key is likely to be the running back on the linebacker's side. Is he going to carry the ball? Is he going to be sent out for a pass? Is he going to block?

The linebacker's third key is the guard on his side. Is he going to block for a run or a pass? Is he going to pull? If he is pulling, is it a sweep or a trap?

How the other guard, the far guard, blocks is important, too.

Sometimes he blocks the tackle, at other times the end, and at still other times he pulls. Each type of block is a clue that the run is coming in a certain direction.

When covering on a pass, a linebacker will seek to read the receiver to get a clue as to which direction the man is going to cut. In Super Bowl V, Mike Curtis intercepted a pass meant for the Cowboys' Dan Reeves in the game's dying minutes, a play that led directly to Baltimore's win. Curtis' man to cover on the play was Bob Hayes. As the two raced downfield together, Curtis read Hayes' eyes. When he saw Hayes glance across the field toward Reeves, it made Curtis realize that the ball wasn't going to Hayes, so he drifted over to Reeves' side of the field. Safety Jerry Logan slammed into Reeves as he went for the ball, it spurted into the air, and Curtis gathered it in before it struck the ground. It wasn't a case of Curtis just happening to be in the right place at the right time; it was shrewdness.

What has been said regarding keying and reacting shouldn't imply that linebackers are always on their own, acting purely as individuals. Not at all. The success of the defensive unit depends on teamwork. The linebackers must work closely with one another, with the members of the secondary, and the linemen.

The basic formation the defensive team uses dictates just how the members of the unit are to cooperate with one another. This formation changes from play to play, depending on the situation.

The basic defensive formation in pro football is the 4-3. Four men are in the line, four are deep. The three linebackers are in between.

But this formation is subject to countless variations. For example, to get defensive strength on the right side, a team may use what is called a 5-right defense. It looks like this:

When a team is backed up to its goal line, it is likely to use what is called a 6-1 defense. The outside linebackers are brought into the line and get into a three-point stance. The idea, of course, is to stop the ball carrier at the line of scrimmage.

The defensive coach on the sidelines, using hand signals, usually calls the defensive formation the team is to use. After taking the signal from the defensive coach, the middle linebacker announces the formation in the defensive team's huddle. He may say, "4-3 weak rotate," or he might say, "4-3, weak safety blitz." The "4-3" tells the linemen and linebackers how to line up, and the phrase "weak safety blitz" informs the defensive players that a blitz is coming and instructs the weak-side safety to

Using hand signals, coach Ernie Stautner calls formations for Dallas defensive unit.

44

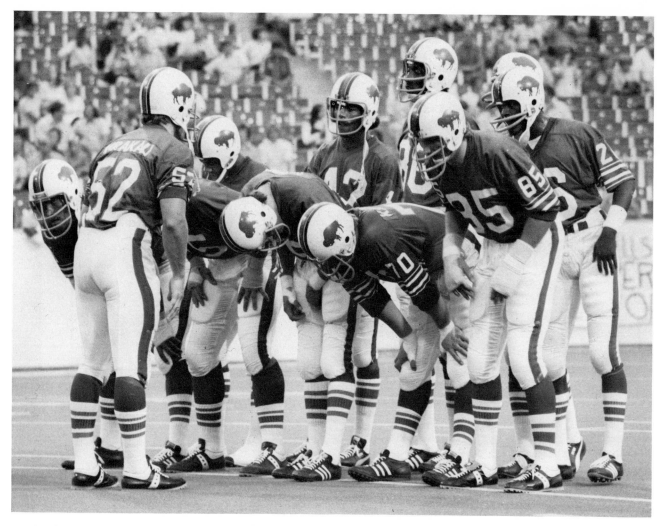

Linebacker Merv Krakau of the Buffalo Bills gives his defensive team colleagues their instructions.

do the blitzing. "Weak rotate" means that the members of the secondary and the linebackers are to slant to the weak side of the field in taking up their coverage posts.

While a team may have twenty or so coverages in its repertoire, they usually draw upon only five or six in a particular game. Some teams use code words in the defensive huddle to indicate the formations to be used.

When the offensive team breaks from the huddle and players line up, the middle linebacker watches carefully. The opposition may use a formation which the defense hasn't anticipated, so it's up to the middle linebacker to rearrange things, that is, call a different formation. This practice is known as calling an audible, or "audibilizing."

Suppose a team is lined up in a conventional 4-3 formation. But as the offense lines up, the middle linebacker reads that a pass is coming. He then changes the position of his tackle, so that the man is opposite the gap between center and guard, which enables the man to rush the passer more effectively. Outside linebackers are often responsible for mov-

Anticipating a pass, the middle linebacker changes the position of the tackle (T), putting him opposite the gap between center and guard.

"Flanker left! Flanker left!," shouts Ron Hornsby.

46

ing the ends in a similar fashion.

For any given game, the defensive team usually has a good idea of what the opposition is going to be doing. The Chicago Bears, for example, have been playing the Green Bay Packers twice a year each year for the last fifty years. Even allowing for personnel and coaching changes, one team develops a "feel" for the other, an intuitive sense of what is going to take place in a given situation. But teams don't depend on intuition, of course. Each works diligently preparing for an opponent, with films and scouting an important part of that preparation.

Coaches use the films and scouting reports to develop frequency charts. These reveal what formations the opposition is likely to use in each one of several game situations—in short yardage and long yardage situations, or when it's first-down-and-ten, second-and-six, third-and-two, and so forth. And the charts also tell what plays the opposition is likely to run from each of the particular formations.

Films are valuable in many ways. Not only do they show the opposition's formations and plays, but they also reveal how personnel react in various situations. Suppose the Raiders are to meet the Chiefs. Kansas City middle linebacker Willie Lanier will study films of the Raiders against some other opponent, the Jets, say. Lanier will pay particular attention to how the Jet middle linebacker played against the Oakland center, the man Lanier will be up against. He may be able to detect cer-

```
BROWNS' DEFENSE VS. RAMS
3rd Down - 3 yds. or less
          Red - 2 times
          6-1 - 2 times

3rd Down - 4-6 yds.

3rd Down - 7 yds. plus
          Preventive defense - 3-4 blue - 2 times
          4-3 Red 88 - 1 time
          4-3 Under 6-1 - 1 time
          Over red - 2 times
          Over blue - 2 times

50% over or under defenses played in this game.

RAMS MOST SUCCESSFUL PLAYS
Runs
          3R - 49HGO +6, +7
Passes
          3 Lt. - Gr. lt. 5 turn +38
          4 Lt. - Br. rt. - 5 comeback +8, +15, +12, +10
          3 Rt. - Gr. - 5 turn +16, +17, +17
          2 Rt. - Br. lt. to 4 flare over +20
          3 Rt. - Gr. 5 comeback +12
          3 Rt. - Gr. rt. 9 & 5 left to 9, +20, +17
          3 Lt. - Gr. 5 & 8 rt. to 5 +15
          4 Lt. - Br. rt. - 8 look out +50
          3 Rt. - 745 - 9 look in +20
```

This information—from a scouting report on the Los Angeles Rams—indicates the team's most successful plays following a game against the Cleveland Browns.

tain weaknesses that he can exploit.

Sometimes during a game, an opponent will do something that no one has anticipated. Teams prepare for this eventuality by stationing coaches and scouts high above the field of play, usually in the press box, and their job is to watch the opposition and report their findings to the bench by telephone.

A Dolphin assistant coach has advice for Nick Buoniconti.

Giant owner Wellington Mara takes Poloroid pictures of enemy formations and tosses them down to his coaches from his seat in a camera cage.

The head coach, from his post on the sidelines, doesn't get a clear picture of what's going on. He sees only bits and pieces of the action. The same is true of the players. They know what is happening right in front of them, but not much else. Sometimes a man will come off the field of play and the first thing he will say is, "What happened?"

Besides the coaches and scouts in the press box,

An assistant at coach George Allen's elbow carefully charts opposition plays and formations.

Linebackers Pat Hughes and Jim Files plan strategy with coach Jim Garrett.

there are assistants on the sidelines who keep charts concerning what formations and plays the opposition is using.

All of this intelligence concerning enemy operation is constantly being fed to the linebackers by a defensive coach. In a close game, there are hurried conferences every time the linebackers come off the field. One of the linebackers may talk by telephone to a coach upstairs. Strategy is changed frequently. Despite the scouting, the films, and all of the time and effort that goes into preparing for an opponent, there is always a great deal of adjustment.

Besides their duties and responsibilities on plays from scrimmage, linebackers are also frequently used on special teams—the punt and punt return teams, the kickoff and kickoff return teams, and the field goal and extra point teams.

On kickoffs and punts, when players are racing toward each other at breakneck speed, injuries are frequent. Indeed, the injury rate on special teams is said to be eight times as great as it is for plays from the line of scrimmage, which is why these units are commonly referred to as "suicide squads." Coaches staff special teams with players who have mobility and a desire for contact. Linebackers, of course, score high in both categories.

Players on special teams fall into one of three different groups. There are the rookies and second-year men who have yet to win a role as either a defensive or offensive regular. Playing on special teams gives them an opportunity to display their skills, their courage, too. "Special teams," Vince Lombardi once said, "will tell you one thing—who wants to hit and who doesn't. And you find out right away."

Special teams also include regulars, players who have what is known as "position ability," that is, they are able to play a number of different roles, not just in the one that happens to be listed after

Nick Buoniconti gets ready to charge Pete Gogolak on Giant point-after attempt.

their name in the game program. Dave Robinson, who has been called the best outside linebacker in the history of the game, played on special teams for the Packers. Nick Buoniconti did for the Dolphins.

Former regulars are a third category of player that comprises special teams. Ike Kelly of the Eagles is a case in point. A starting linebacker for the Eagles for many years, Kelly lost his job to a younger man, but remained with the club as a special-team player.

That linebackers play on special teams shouldn't be considered unusual. The assignment is included in the basic description of what a linebacker is supposed to do, namely, everything.

Ike Kelley (51) was special team star for the Philadelphia Eagles.

STOPPING THE RUN

On running plays, linebackers have one simple assignment: make the tackle.

How they make it really doesn't matter. Because there's so much happening at the line of scrimmage, so many bodies in the way, often the only thing a linebacker can do is reach out and make a grab, hoping to get an arm, a leg, a foot, or maybe a handful of jersey. Nick Buoniconti once brought down a ball carrier by holding onto the man's shoelace, slowing him down until a teammate could come over and help out.

The shoelace tackle is a rarity, however. Linebackers have to be sure tacklers, jolting tacklers. Big, strong linebackers, such as Dave Robinson, hit the ball carrier shoulder high and drive him into the ground. Smaller men usually have to hit lower, thigh-high or knee-high.

Bull-necked Tommy Nobis of the Atlanta Falcons goes for the ball carrier headfirst. "Your first contact is with your head," he says. "That's the way my high school coach taught me—hit 'em in the goozle [the chest]."

Willie Lanier of the Kansas City Chiefs used to be a headfirst tackler, but not any more. In a game against the Denver Broncos, he dove for the ball carrier, aiming his helmet for the man's belly.

Opposite: **Bills' John Skorupan (55) targets on Duane Thomas.**

53

While Lanier was in midair, one of the runner's knees struck him on the forehead, and his helmet only partially took the blow. Lanier staggered about the field woozily, then collapsed. Doctors found he had suffered a severe concussion. When he recovered, and started playing again, Lanier changed his style.

The more accepted method of tackling is to get one's head *and* shoulder into the ball carrier, then slam him to the ground. But even this style subjects the tackler to a certain amount of punishment. Joe Schmidt, middle linebacker for the Detroit Lions for thirteen seasons, who used this method, often

Despite the crowd, Giants' Pat Hughes manages to stop Calvin Hill in accepted fashion.

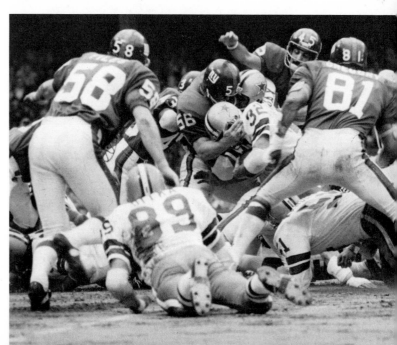

Nick Buoniconti (85) throws himself in front of Ron Johnson to bring him down.

jokes about its effects. He says that when he went into pro football he was 6-foot-3; when he retired, 5-foot-11. All those seasons of using his upper body like a battering ram had cost him his neck, which had been pounded down between his shoulders.

Tough Dave Wilcox of the San Francisco 49ers has an ususual method of stopping the ball carrier. He likes to grab hold of the runner by his upper arms and then twist the man to the ground, the way a cowboy wrestles a steer down. "Dave doesn't always do it this way, just when he has someone trapped," said Dick Nolan, coach of the 49ers. "He's so strong in the arms and shoulders he can get away with it."

While making tackles is what the linebacker gets paid for, a good part of his afternoon is spent avoiding blockers. He can't allow himself to get involved in a wrestling match with a blocker. Any delay, even a second, means extra yardage for the man with the ball. The idea is to go at the blocker and "pop" him, take control, and then move on to the ball carrier.

The linebacker's chief weapon is the hand shiver. As the blocker lunges for him, the linebacker slams the man's shoulder pads or helmet with the heels of his hands. If the blocker is coming in low, he'll slam him down. If he's belt high, he'll try to straighten him up. The forearms can also be used to deliver a shiver.

Dave Robinson swung his forearm like a club at enemy players. "The harder you hit a man in the first period," he once said, "the more you slow him down in the fourth period. Also, the harder you hit someone, the less it hurts you."

This is what Dick Butkus uses to ward off enemy blockers.

If the play is coming for the linebacker head-on, and he needs more power than his hands or forearms can provide, he hits into the blocker with his shoulder, trying to force him to the right or left.

There are several types of blocks the linebacker has to deal with. There is the hook block, for instance. When a player executes a hook block, what he does is screen off the linebacker from the play. Suppose a team calls a running play to the left side. The tight end will then line up on that side, and as the ball is snapped he'll charge to the linebacker's right side, but instead of trying to bowl him over he'll simply stand erect and shield him out of the play.

If the linebacker gives ground or tries to fight the tight end, the running back will streak for long yardage. The linebacker has to be able to anticipate the play and shoot through to either make the tackle or spill the blocker.

The crackback block is another weapon used against linebackers. It's an insidious method of attack, looked upon in somewhat the same way the bean ball is in baseball. Any player on the defensive unit can be the victim of a crackback block, but when the linebacker is the target it's usually a wide receiver who delivers it. The receiver drifts to the outside as if he's running a pass pattern, then suddenly cuts back to the inside to ambush the unsuspecting linebacker, hitting him low, about knee-high.

Dallas linebacker Chuck Howley was struck down by a crackback block delivered by Charley Taylor of the Washington Redskins during the 1972 season. Cartilage and ligaments on Howley's left knee were torn to shreds. "The crackback isn't football," says one player. "It's mayhem." Rules regarding the crackback were revised for the 1974 season, with wide receivers prohibited from blocking below the waist.

As these comments imply, the linebacker is never really certain who is going to be blocking him. The middle linebacker, for instance, knows that normally the center will be assigned to take him out, but he has to be wary that a guard isn't given the job.

The center, instead of blocking the linebacker, will slant to one side and block the tackle (see diagram). The guard, as soon as the center crosses in front of him, fires out to hit the linebacker. This is known as cross-blocking.

The linebacker can thwart this strategy by slam-

Normally, it's the center who blocks the middle linebacker, but a tackle can also be assigned to do the job (right).

ming into the hole created by the center. This enables him to stop the run if it's aimed for the hole or help smother a pass attempt, but the linebacker has to move quickly and decisively. A moment's hesitation and he gets thumped by the guard.

While every team has scores of running plays in its repertoire, there are three basic ways in which the offense attacks on the ground. A team will strike

On this off-tackle slant, the running back set to the left (R) delivers a key block on the outside linebacker (O), nudging him to the left. This allows the ball carrier to cut in behind. The wide receiver (W) contains the cornerback (C).

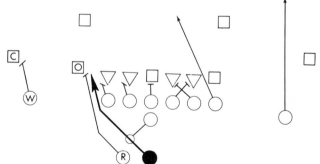

at the center of the line with dive plays, toward the end with slants, or around the ends with sweeps.

On the dive play, the ball carrier can head straight up the middle or veer to either the right or left of center. The off-tackle slant is also used in short yardage situations. After taking the handoff, the running back veers to the right or left, then hits into the line just outside tackle.

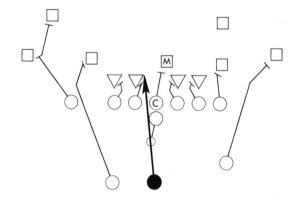

On this dive play, the center (C) blocks the middle linebacker (M) to the right. If he's successful, the ball carrier goes left.

On the sweep, the guards pull from their position in the line to lead the blocking, first running laterally, then turning downfield. The middle and outside linebacker must work together to stop the play. The outside man's job is to steer the play inside,

Giants' Doug Van Horn (63) clears away the linebacker as Ron Johnson sweeps to the left.

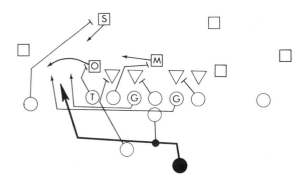

This is a typical sweep, the running back getting the quarterback's handoff and heading left behind a pair of blocking guards (G). The key man in stopping the play is the outside linebacker (O). He must fight off the tight end (T), then force the play inside, so the middle linebacker (M) or safety (S) can make the tackle.

with the safety on that side coming up to fill his coverage area. If the outside linebacker does his job, he forces the ball carrier right into the arms of the middle linebacker. "You should make the tackle on this play every time," says Dick Butkus.

Middle linebackers stop more running plays than the outside men. But the number of tackles a man makes isn't necessarily evidence of his true worth.

After all, the middle linebacker is, by the nature of his position, in the middle of things. If he stood around with his hands on his hips all day, he'd still be in on a good number of plays.

Where a man makes his tackles is significant. A linebacker should barrel in and stop the ball carrier at the line of scrimmage. Mike Lucci, who played the middle for the Detroit Lions, made his share of tackles, but was criticized for not moving quickly enough, for allowing the ball carrier four or five yards before he brings him down.

The most notable example of misevaluation in the case of a linebacker concerned one Wahoo McDaniel, who played for the New York Jets in 1964. McDaniel was a hard hitter, but he lacked mobility and was ineffective against most passes and runs to the outside. His greatest asset was his whimsical nickname. Whenever he made a tackle, and he made more than a few because the Jet line was sievelike in those days, the public address announcer would call out, "Tackle by Waaaa-hoooo." The fans roared in delight. By the end of the season, no Jet player was as popular as Wahoo. Among the fans, that is. The coaches knew better. They traded Wahoo away before the next season began.

STOPPING THE PASS

In the glory days of the Green Bay Packers during the 1960's, one of quarterback Bart Starr's favorite plays was a long pass to running back Jimmy Taylor. More than once the play resulted in an important touchdown.

It went like this: Starr would send the tight end speeding downfield on a fly pattern to draw the safety deep. The wide receiver in the right side would run a square-in pattern, so as to occupy the cornerback. Taylor, set to the right side, would delay a second, giving the receivers time to clear the area, then circle to the outside and break downfield.

The outside linebacker would pick up Taylor as he came toward him. But Taylor was fast and could often beat the man. And even if he couldn't outdistance the linebacker, he was strong enough to out-wrestle him for the ball.

You don't see quarterbacks throwing long passes to their running backs any more. Indeed, you hardly ever see them throwing long passes to anyone. The reason you don't is the zone defense.

As Giants' tight end Bob Tucker drifts downfield, Redskins' Jack Pardee comes up to defend.

When a linebacker reads a pass is coming, he hustles into his zone, and he's already there by the time the running back arrives. Should the back race deep, the linebacker lets him go, knowing that a speedy safety or cornerback will come up to cover him.

Virtually all teams today use a zone pass defense, which means that each of the three linebackers (and the four deep backs as well) are assigned a specific area of the field to cover. This is in contrast to the man-to-man defense, which used to be in vogue. With the man-to-man, each defensive player had a particular receiver to cover and he stayed with that man no matter where he went.

The man-to-man system was difficult—and that is putting it mildly—for the linebackers. The quarterback would try to isolate a very fast receiver on a not-so-fast linebacker, and then send the man sprinting for the end zone. The linebacker couldn't keep pace. Imagine Willie Lanier or Dick Butkus trying to cover someone like O. J. Simpson over a stretch of 20 or 30 yards. It wouldn't even be close.

The zone defense solves this problem. It means that the linebacker has to stay with the receiver only while the man is crossing through the linebacker's zone. When the speed merchant gets deep, someone else, a safety or a cornerback, a man who is likely to be as fleet-footed as the receiver, is there to pick him up.

Teams use several different types of zones, but

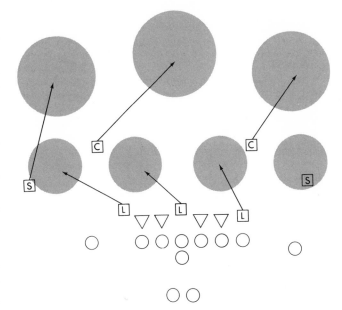

The rotating zone

the rotating zone and the double zone are the ones that are used the most. In the rotating zone, there are four short zones and three deep zones (see diagram). The three linebackers, plus one of the cornerbacks, cover the short zones. The other members of the defensive secondary—the two safeties and the other cornerback—dart back to cover deep.

In the example shown here, the defensive players are slanting in a clockwise direction. They can also move counterclockwise. In either case, they appear to be "rotating" and, hence, the name.

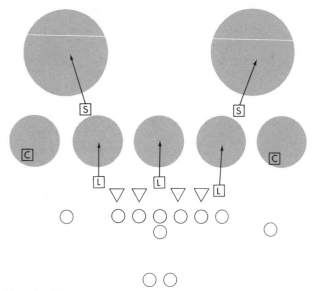

The double zone

In the double zone, there are five zones short and two deep (see diagram). Again, the linebackers cover the short zones, as do the two cornerbacks. The safeties cover the deep zones.

As the quarterback drifts back to throw, the linebacker backpedals into his zone, alert to pick up a receiver. Maybe it will be one of the wide receivers, maybe the tight end, or even one of the running backs—it doesn't matter.

The rules say that you cannot block an eligible receiver once the ball is in the air. But *before* the ball is thrown, there is plenty a linebacker can do.

Linebackers are taught to jam the receiver, to meet him head-on and slam him on the shoulder pads, straightening him up. A man can't run fast when he's erect. At the same time he's jamming the receiver, the linebacker has to keep his eyes on what's happening in the backfield. It could be that the quarterback is sending a second man, a back, circling into his zone, so the linebacker can't get too involved with the first one.

Chuck Howley of the Dallas Cowboys was outstanding in the way he covered pass receivers. One thing that made him so efficient was his unpredictability. When a back swept into his coverage zone, Howley might force him to go to the outside a couple of times. But the next time the man circled out, Howley would force him inside, taking the outside away. The receiver and the quarterback never quite knew what Howley was going to do, and there would be a moment of hesitation as a result. It's moments of hesitation that cause plays to fail.

Some linebackers have a talent for playing "off" a receiver, that is, luring the quarterback into throwing to the man, then roaring up to make the interception. Chris Hanburger of the Redskins has the savvy to do this, also the speed. He had four interceptions in 1972, the most of any NFC linebacker.

***Opposite:* The zone defense was thwarted here, as Jets' Rich Caster gets set to grab Joe Namath's pass. Mike Kolen of the Dolphins (57) is the victim.**

Chuck Howley of the Cowboys delays Don Hermann while keeping a watchful eye on the quarterback.

Of course, linebackers don't intercept as many passes as the safeties or cornerbacks do. After all, the linebackers cover the short zones, and passes that enter these zones are usually traveling at bullet-speed. About all the linebacker can do is lunge at the ball, hoping to deflect it. But linebackers affect many passes—many more than they get credit for —by tipping the ball, by reaching up and grazing it

A pass interception put this grin on Chuck Howley's face.

Nick Buoniconti practices intercepting.

with their finger tips as it sails deep. This causes the ball to veer off course, and the result can be an incompletion or maybe even an interception.

LINEBACKER INTERCEPTIONS
All-Time Season Records

8—Bulldog Turner, Chicago Bears (1942)
7—Don Shinnick, Baltimore Colts (1959)
7—Vince Costello, Cleveland Browns (1963)

A team needs more than simply an efficient zone defense to throttle down the opposition's passing attack. What the linebackers and deep men do has to be coordinated with a strong rush by the linemen, the front four. Not pressuring the passer usually leads to a calamity. It is generally agreed that any skilled and experienced quarterback can complete a pass if given sufficient time, sufficient time being something more than three or four seconds. After all, the quarterback knows in advance where he is going to throw the ball; the receivers know where they're supposed to run. The defensive players can only react, which puts them at a disadvantage, and the more time the receivers have to act out their roles, the more disadvantageous the situation becomes.

There's another way of putting pressure on the passer besides having the front four rush. It's by

Linebacker Brian Kelley of the Giants races for the end zone following an interception.

blitzing, by having one or more of the linebackers charge across the line of scrimmage at the snap of the ball in an attempt to deck the quarterback. When the blitz is successful, it not only destroys the play but it can result in a loss of yardage or even a fumble.

But to blitz is to gamble. It leaves one or more gaps in the defense (depending on how many players go in), and a sharp quarterback can exploit these weaknesses with a quick pass. Of course, the defense is hoping that the linebacker will get to the quarterback before he can get the ball away, or at least force him to throw hurriedly.

Sometimes a linebacker will blitz from his normal set position after the ball is snapped. The other method is for the linebacker to move nearer to the line of scrimmage and, anticipating the snap, rip through as the center puts the ball into the quarterback's hands. The presence of the linebacker at the line of scrimmage doesn't go unnoticed. The quarterback sees him and so does the center, and so do the other members of the offensive line, particularly the man who's been assigned to block the blitzer, probably a guard. Thus, by moving up into the line, the linebacker can cause the guard to hesitate momentarily before he blocks his usual man. It is these split seconds of delay that give one man an advantage over another.

There are many different kinds of blitzes. There is what some teams refer to as a double blitz, in which the middle linebacker and one of the outside men pour in. Sometimes the two outside men shoot in and the man in the middle remains back. Other times all three rush in. Then there is the safety blitz. In this, not only the linebackers but one of the safeties go blazing through. The safety blitz had better work, however, because, with so many men pouring in, it makes for acres of open space out there.

It's up to the defensive linemen to open up holes for the blitzers. For example, when the defensive end takes the lineman opposite him to the outside, he creates an opening inside—and the blitzer shoots through. If he takes the man inside, the linebacker goes outside.

The linebackers have to be careful not to tip off that they're planning to blitz. The quarterback is trying to read their intentions. If it's a certain passing situation and the linebackers are going to be dropping back to cover their zones, they may "cheat" a step or two, that is, begin edging toward their zones before the ball is snapped. But if they're going to be blitzing, they may cheat in the other direction, toward their holes. It's like getting a head start in a footrace. An astute quarterback can perceive these clues and, thus, anticipate the blitz. So the linebackers have to be actors, giving indications that they're going to be dropping back when actually they're planning to rush in.

Even the way the linebacker sets his feet can be a tip-off. If he always puts his right foot in front of his left when he's going to blitz, the opposition is likely to notice the habit from studying game films. You can't allow yourelf to develop any tendencies. You have to keep mixing up what you do.

Blitzing is also known as red-dogging, a term

first used in 1949. That year the Chicago Bears had a running back named Ed (Catfoot) Cody, who backed up the line on defense. One day in a game against the Chicago Cardinals, Cody decided to improvise. As the ball was snapped, he bolted across the line of scrimmage and into the offensive backfield of the Cards, where he got his hands on quarterback Paul Christman and wrestled him to the ground. The Cardinal linemen, who were unfamiliar

Dick Butkus (51) is held up at the line of scrimmage, but Doug Buffone (55) blitzes through. Patriot's Jim Plunkett is his target.

with such goings-on, made little or no attempt to stop Cody.

A few plays later, Cody tried it a second time. Again, no one tried to stop him, and again he flattened poor Christman. So it went through the afternoon. No less than thirteen times Cody charged across the line, and each time he hammered Christman to the ground. After the game, Hunk Anderson, a coach for the Bears, remarked, "That Cody looked like a mad dog coming through there."

Anderson saw the value of Cody's tactics and realized that they could be performed with several variations. In the weeks that followed, he formalized the rushes of the "mad dogs," developing code names to designate who would rush. When only one of the linebackers went in, the play was to be known as a "white dog." When two linebackers went, a "blue dog." When all three linebackers charged, Anderson called it a "red dog." In time, the term "red dog" came to apply to any charge across the line of scrimmage by any one or all of the linebackers, or by any member of the defensive secondary.

Some teams used to blitz frequently, as often as 10 to 15 per cent of the time. Not any more. One reason the use of the blitz has slackened is because

In the heyday of the blitz, New York Giants followed these instructions when "shooting" linebackers. Page is from a team playbook.

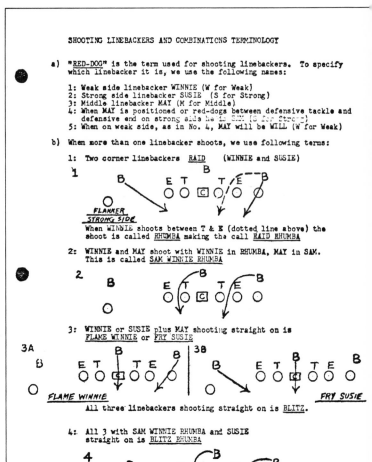

SHOOTING LINEBACKERS AND COMBINATIONS TERMINOLOGY

a) "RED-DOG" is the term used for shooting linebackers. To specify which linebacker it is, we use the following names:

1: Weak side linebacker WINNIE (W for Weak)
2: Strong side linebacker SUSIE (S for Strong)
3: Middle linebacker MAY (M for Middle)
4: When MAY is positioned or red-dogs between defensive tackle and defensive end on strong side he is SAM (S for Strong)
5: When on weak side, as in No. 4, MAY will be WILL (W for Weak)

b) When more than one linebacker shoots, we use following terms:

1: Two corner linebackers RAID (WINNIE and SUSIE)

FLANKER
STRONG SIDE

When WINNIE shoots between T & E (dotted line above) the shoot is called RHUMBA making the call RAID RHUMBA

2: WINNIE and MAY shoot with WINNIE in RHUMBA, MAY in SAM. This is called SAM WINNIE RHUMBA

3: WINNIE or SUSIE plus MAY shooting straight on is FLAME WINNIE or FRY SUSIE

FLAME WINNIE   FRY SUSIE

All three linebackers shooting straight on is BLITZ.

4: All 3 with SAM WINNIE RHUMBA and SUSIE straight on is BLITZ RHUMBA

It's no fun to be a blitz victim. Here Archie Manning is treated rudely by Jets' Ralph Baker.

of what happened in Super Bowl III in January, 1969. The game matched the Colts and the Jets.

The Colts went into the game as 16-point favorites. They had won thirteen of fourteen league games, largely because of their rock-ribbed defense which had shut out four opponents and tied the NFL record for fewest-points-allowed. One of the team's most effective weapons was a devastating blitz, one that usually involved the safeties, Rick Volk and Jerry Logan, as well as at least one of the linebackers.

Jet quarterback Joe Namath had no fear of Baltimore's blitzing tactics. He had watched films of the Colts and noticed the big gaps that resulted whenever they shot a safety or linebacker through. He knew he could take advantage of these openings. "I just prayed the Colts *would* blitz," said Namath. "If they did, they were dead."

In the game's second period, neither team having scored, the Jets took over the ball after a Baltimore drive had bogged down. With it second-and-10 on the New York 48, Namath pedaled back to throw and in blitzed the Colts. But Namath, reading his keys masterfully, saw the blitz coming, and before anyone could lay a hand on him, he rifled the ball to George Sauer for a 14-yard gain. Three plays later, the Colt linebackers ripped in again. But again

Namath picked it up, this time lofting a short pass to Matt Snell sprinting out of the backfield. The Jets scored soon after, setting the stage for one of pro football's most notable upsets. The reputation of the blitz was never quite the same.

A number of things influence a team's decision whether or not to blitz. A young quarterback is certain to be tested by blitzers. Perhaps they won't touch him, but they may be able to intimidate him, causing him to spring back from the center too quickly, fumbling as a result. Or maybe the young man will throw too quickly or while he's off balance, and the ball will be intercepted.

The skill of the quarterback is a factor. A man who has a weak arm or lacks in accuracy doesn't see many blitzes. Why bother? The defense figures. Let him throw.

Some teams don't blitz because the coaches feel that their players are skilled enough and strong enough to hold the opposition. In other words, there's no reason to gamble. Yet you still see the blitz, and it can be a telling piece of strategy. In an NFC play-off game in 1972, Washington's Chris Hanburger leaped over a blocker to land on Roger Staubach, throwing him for a big loss. It was a critical play in a game that boosted the Redskins into the Super Bowl.

COUNTERS, DRAWS, AND OTHER PROBLEMS

Quickness and speed are two qualities every linebacker must have. But not too much quickness nor too much speed.

Take what happened in Super Bowl VI, the Dallas Cowboys vs. the Miami Dolphins. Nick Buoniconti, a ten-year veteran, was the middle linebacker for the Dolphins. "Small but quick, darting, intelligent" was the way that Buoniconti was described in the game program.

But Super Bowl VI was a black day for Buoniconti. Realizing that he was the key to the Miami defense, Dallas went into the game with plays especially designed to turn Buoniconti's quickness against him and thereby neutralize his effectiveness.

The basis of the Cowboy strategy was the counter play. One of the Dallas running backs, either Duane Thomas or Walt Garrison, usually the former, would take the handoff from the quarterback, then head to one side, the right side, say. Buoniconti would break to the right, too. Then one of the Dallas linemen, or sometimes the other back, would nudge Buoniconti even more to the right. Thomas, the ball carrier, reading what was happening, would suddenly cut back in the opposite direction, then rip off tackle or up the middle for a long gain. About all that Buoniconti could do was watch him go by.

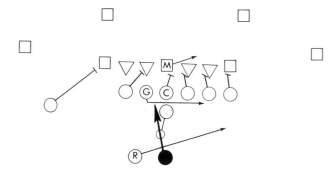

In the counter play, the defense is made to think that the ball is going in one direction; the runner is then sent in the direction opposite. Here the flow of the play looks to be to the right with a guard (G) pulling and heading to the right, and a running back (R) slanting in that direction. When the middle linebacker (M) takes a step or two to the right, the center (C) slams into him, sending him farther in that direction. The back then takes the handoff and heads to the left.

It must be said that Nick Buoniconti wasn't the only Dolphin to turn in a below-par performance that afternoon. The Cowboys rushed for 252 yards, a Super Bowl record, which suggests that several members of the Miami defensive team must have been out to lunch. As for the Miami offense, it wasn't able to generate enough steam to score a touchdown, something that had never happened in the Super Bowl before.

Buoniconti offered no excuses for what happened. "They waited for me to commit myself," he recalls.

"Then the blocker would take me where I wanted to go, and the back would make his cut the other way." Looking back, Buoniconti feels that his preparation for the game put too much stress on formations and not enough on the type of blocking used in the line. "We were off that one important step that makes the difference between making the play and getting nothing," he says.

If playing the position of linebacker were exactly as described in the preceding chapters, it wouldn't be too difficult. Read a pass is coming, and you drop back and cover your zone. When it's a run, fight off the blocking and make the tackle. But it's much more complicated than these statements imply. The problem is that the offense is always working to mask its intentions. The quarterback tries to get the linebackers to read one thing, then does something entirely different.

Besides the counter, another standard method of deception is the draw play, sometimes referred to as the delay. The draw is a running play that looks like a pass at the beginning. The linebackers see the quarterback take the snap, drift back, and set up, scanning downfield for a receiver. They see the offensive lineman stand erect to pass block. So the linebackers do what they think they're supposed to do, drop into their coverage zone.

But suddenly the quarterback hands off to a running back, and the man charges into the line. If the middle linebacker has not played alertly, ruling out

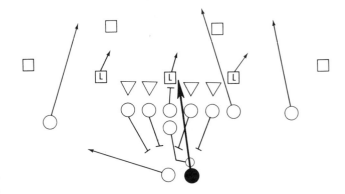

In this draw play, the blockers give ground as if blocking for a pass, and the quarterback retreats as if he is going to throw. The linebackers (L) drop back, looking for the pass. But suddenly the quarterback hands off to a running back, who charges into the line.

the draw before taking his drop, the damage can be considerable—five or six yards.

The center plays a vital role in the draw. After he delays, he must drive into the middle linebacker. The right guard helps create the hole by blocking the defensive tackle, either to the inside or outside. The ball carrier reads the blocking and reacts accordingly.

In order to stop the play, the middle linebacker must read the center's delay and block, a tip-off to what's coming. He shouts out, "Draw! Draw! Draw!" At the same time, he fights off the center and piles into the ball carrier, either hauling him to the ground or slowing him sufficiently so that his teammates can come up and finish the job. On the draw, as on so many other plays, the linebacker's warning yell is of crucial importance.

A variation of the standard draw play is the quarterback draw. Instead of handing off to a running back, the quarterback simply tucks the ball to his belly and does the rushing himself. The play is considered too much of a hazard for most quarterbacks, but Roger Staubach of the Cowboys and Greg Larsen of the Lions try it occasionally.

What makes any draw play especially difficult is that the linebacker is three or four yards deep when the ball carrier finally gets the ball and, thus, an easy target for the center or other offensive lineman. Dick Butkus says that the draw is one of the two toughest plays with which a linebacker must cope. The other, says Butkus, is the screen pass.

The screen pass works like this: With the snap of the ball, the offensive linemen begin retreating and the quarterback goes back as if to throw. The linebackers read pass and head for their zones.

The quarterback stops, fakes a pass, then retreats some more. The offensive linemen on one side release their blocks and dart toward the sideline to set up a "screen" of blockers. Just behind the screen there's a running back, and he reaches up to take a short toss from the quarterback.

When the screen pass works as the offense hopes, the outside linebacker has two or three 240-pound

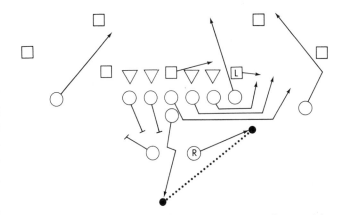

The screen pass puts enormous pressure on the outside linebacker (L). He has to topple or knife through a wall of blockers in order to get to the running back (R), who is the target for the quarterback's pass.

linemen bearing down on him, with the ball carrier right behind. The linebacker has to get help in order to be able to stop the play.

A linebacker who happens to be small and quick can have an advantage over a big man in such a situation. Larry Grantham of the Jets, for example, who weighed a mere 205 pounds, had a talent for being able to knife in between blockers to bring down the man with the ball.

The middle linebacker can sometimes diagnose the screen pass by reading the blocking in the line. The linemen, in their haste to get to the outside, sometimes fail to fake in a believable manner. As soon as the linebacker reads a screen pass is com-

Franco Harris of the Steelers goes for distance with a screen pass.

ing, he's supposed to shout a warning to his teammates.

The outside linebackers key on the running backs. When one of them delays, it can be a clue that the screen is coming. They also keep an eye on the blocking in the line.

74

Opposite: **Larry Grantham of the New York Jets was skilled at breaking up the screen pass. Here he leaps to nail the fleet O. J. Simpson.**

"You can stop the screen by yourself if you can recognize it quick enough," said Dick Butkus. "Otherwise, you have to have help. You've got three linemen coming at you and you've got to come up with a really great play to stop the ball carrier alone."

The draw play looks like a pass, but it's a run. Then there's the opposite, the play that begins as a run but it's really a pass. It's called the play-action pass. It's seen frequently nowadays.

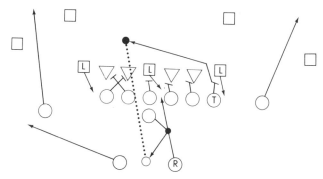

Here is a typical play-action pass. The blockers fire out as if a running play is coming. The quarterback fakes a handoff to a running back (R), who hits into the line. The linebackers (L) charge in. But it's a pass— the quarterback throwing to the tight end (T), who has slanted into the area vacated by the middle linebacker.

Philadelphia quarterback John Reaves fakes a handoff to running back Po James.

When using play-action, the offensive linemen fire out as if a run were coming. The quarterback takes the pass from center, turns, and puts the ball into the belly of a running back, and he slams into the line. But the man doesn't have the ball; the quarterback never releases it. Concealing the ball at his thigh, he darts back to throw.

Whether the pass that ensues is good or not usually depends on whether the linebackers have taken the fake. If they are deceived and rush up in an effort to stop the run, or if they merely hold their ground, there is going to be plenty of open space for the receivers.

Dave Robinson once recalled that in his rookie year quarterbacks fooled him constantly with play-action passes. "There were always acres of grass in front of me," he said.

Later he learned to "feel things." "I'd see one, two, three keys that would say run, but I'd 'feel' pass. Then I'd see the last key and I would know I was right. It would be a pass."

Linebackers learn to watch the quarterback's hands, and they try to determine whether he is using one hand or both of them in making the handoff. If the quarterback keeps both hands on the ball, it may be an indication he's going to keep the ball, that it's a play-action pass. It's difficult for some quarterbacks to execute a fake when using only one hand.

Another type of pass intended to trap the line-

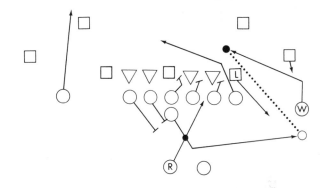

The left linebacker (L) is the victim on this rollout. The quarterback, after faking a handoff to a running back (R), rolls to his right, watching the left linebacker as he goes. When the linebacker charges in to make the tackle, the quarterback loops the ball over the man's head to the wide receiver (W).

backers, one of the outside linebackers especially, is the rollout. This, like the draw play, can begin with a fake plunge into the line by a running back. But the principal role is played by the quarterback. He races to one side after getting the snap, his arm raised to throw.

When the quarterback scampers laterally, the linebacker on that side goes with him. When the quarterback gets set to throw, the linebacker must decide what to do—cover the receiver or go after the quarterback. But either decision can be wrong. If the linebacker decides to stay with the receiver, the quarterback is likely to tuck the ball under his

Rolling out—this is Craig Morton of the Cowboys.

arm and run with it. But suppose the linebacker decides to take off after the quarterback. Then the man can loop the ball over the linebacker's head to the receiver.

The halfback option is similar to the rollout in that it puts the outside linebacker under severe pressure. The quarterback hands off to a running back, who circles to one side, reading the defensive coverage as he goes. Depending on how the linebacker and safety react, the back either runs or throws.

Usually the linebacker plays the halfback option as a run, driving in to force the issue, that is, making the halfback throw the ball. This puts the pressure on the strong-side safety. When the halfback swings out of the backfield, the safety reads "run" and darts forward. This is what the offense anticipates and sends the tight end in behind. The safety has to recover and hustle back to his zone of coverage. The quicker the linebacker can make the opposition decide on a course of action, the better.

Of course, these aren't the only plays that linebackers have to worry about. There are literally hundreds of others. But these are the ones that are especially designed to deceive the linebackers. Avoiding deception is how they earn their money.

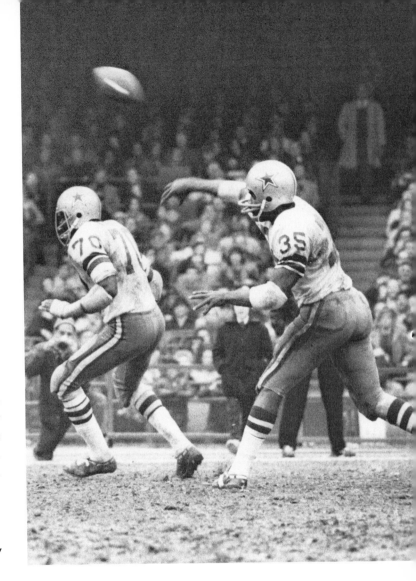

The Dallas Cowboys like to use the halfback option, with Calvin Hill doing the throwing—or running.

TRAINING CAMP

Say "July" to the average person, and it conjures up the hot summer sun, television reruns, school vacation, days at the beach and getting tanned. It often means baseball—playing it, watching the standings, or going to games.

But not if you're in pro football. To players and coaches, July means training camp, when the season actually begins.

Training camp is no vacation. It means scrimmaging—really hitting—on a dusty field in the summer heat. It means calisthenics and running, running when you're too tired to run. It means living in a bleak dorm, team meetings, studying your playbook, and watching films. It's the whole business of getting ready.

Training camps are based at small-town colleges and the off-the-field setting is pleasant and serene. But most players don't like the idea of training camp and some have a hatred for it.

This is especially true for the rookies and marginal players, those who are unsure of their jobs. To these men, training camp represents a time of terrible uncertainty, with one's career hinging on every test of speed, strength, and football ability. You either make the team or you don't. The pressure is enormous.

Not all training camps are the same, however. There are philosophical differences which reflect the attitudes of the head coach and his staff. Some camps are strict and there's a rigid system of discipline. Workouts feature hitting. "They're looking to beat the hell out of you and toughen you up," is the way one player puts it. But at other camps, while the coaches expect players to get ready both physically and mentally, there's more of an emphasis on teaching and learning.

Most teams invite from 60 to 70 players to camp. By the last week in August each squad must be down to 49 players. The final cut is scheduled during the second week in September, just before the opening of the season, when the squad must be down to 40 players.

The first weeks of training are the most rigorous, with two workouts a day scheduled, one in the morning, one in the afternoon. After breakfast, players report to the fieldhouse for taping, then break into small groups—offensive linemen, defensive linemen, linebackers, receivers, and so on—to discuss plays and formations and sometimes view films. The assistant coach in charge of each position conducts the meetings.

Then the players take to the field. All camps feature running, usually sprints. At the beginning of camp, players are timed in the 40-yard dash. A timing of 4.8 or 4.9 seconds is considered good for a linebacker. Players run several 40-yard dashes at the conclusion of each practice session.

At some camps, coaches time players in the one-

Jet linebackers in a training camp sprint.

mile run. At the training camp of the San Diego Chargers, coach Sid Gillman once set a time limit of 6:30 in the mile run, and then instructed players, rookies and veterans alike, to run the distance each day until each man had achieved the standard. Not only was Gillman seeking to improve the cardiovascular system of each player, but he wanted to get an idea of what shape each man was in.

A 6:30 mile is no problem for a wide receiver or a cornerback. Many players in these positions have college experience in track, and are capable of bettering even 5:30. Running backs have no difficulty with the 6:30 mile either.

For linemen, however, it's a different matter. While most have catlike quickness and show good speed over short distances, a mile run against the

Players unlimber—flex—before workout.

clock is a formidable challenge. Walt Sweeney, San Diego's All-Pro guard had misgivings about the test. "If Sid says we'll run the mile every day until we qualify, then I'll jog it in 20 minutes every day until December," Sweeney said.

As for linebackers, most were able to better the prescribed time, but only by a few seconds. Linebacker Rich Redman turned in a time of 6:25;

Pete Barnes had 6:26.

Coaches and trainers have long recognized the importance of strength and endurance, but in recent years they have also begun to emphasize flexibility. The major muscle groups of the body must be stretched daily, it's now realized, in order to prevent the muscles from shortening and tightening. By maintaining an overall suppleness, muscle injuries are sharply reduced.

In recognition of the importance of this phase of training and conditioning, the Pittsburgh Steelers signed Paul Uram as a full-time flexibility coach in 1973. Instead of performing conventional calisthenics before a game, the Steelers stretch. Uram's knowledge of his specialty was acquired as a gymnast. He was first a participant, later a coach. Gymnastics is a sport in which the performer must be totally prepared before competing. Other teams have flex coaches, too, although they have additional duties and responsibilities.

There are many types of specialized equipment strewn about the training camp practice field, each one meant to help a player improve a particular skill. Players seek to enhance their agility by means of the snake drill. The "snake" itself looks like a long black rubber pipe. Hundreds of thin rubber spikes, each about the diameter of a lead pencil, jut out from it. The idea is to move from one end of the snake to the other as fast as possible without stepping on any of the spikes.

Then there's the tackling machine, which consists of a tall and heavy tripod to which is fixed a long steel arm. A tackling dummy is spring-mounted on the arm. Players line up and face the dummy. A coach releases the spring mechanism and the dummy sails toward the man at the head of the line. He must charge into the dummy, hit it hard, stop it, drive it back.

Linebackers use the blocking sled to develop their quickness and ability to react and to hit. A sled consists of a sturdy metal frame fitted with heavy padding and mounted on a runner system of one type or another. When struck, the sled "gives" or slides. A sled drill lasts about ten minutes. Players line up and face the sled, and on the command of "Go!" from the coach, each man launches his body into the sled, striking it with a shoulder or forearm.

There are also two-man sleds and seven-man sleds. Linebackers and other defensive players often use the seven-man sled for what is known as a "butt drill." The players line up opposite one of the endmost pads. On "Go!" the first player explodes into the pad, recoils, then rolls over so he is opposite the adjacent pad, explodes into *it*, recoils, and so on, until he reaches the other end of the sled. Two or three or more players can be involved in hitting the sled at the same time.

Coaches seek to improve linebackers' reactions through what are known as "wave drills." No special equipment is needed. Two or more players take

a ready stance side by side and facing a coach who holds a football out in front of his body, or the coach may hold the ball to the ground as a center does. When the coach suddenly moves the ball to the right, the players quickly break to the right. When the ball goes left, the players do. Or when the coach thrusts the ball out in front of his body, the linebackers backpedal.

Linebackers have to be able to move backward almost as quickly as they do forward. In another backpedaling drill, two linebackers line up side by side facing a coach. On "Go!" they start going backward as fast as they can. The coach passes the ball in between the two men and they grapple for it.

Coach Ed Biles conducts a wave drill.

At noontime, the players have lunch, then rest. At 2:30 P.M., they're back in the fieldhouse for taping and more meetings. Frequently films are screened. These may be films of the previous day's scrimmages or sometimes they are films of an opponent the team is going to face in a preseason game.

Much of the time in these meetings is given over to a discussion of tactics and strategy. Linebackers are drilled on the team's defensive formations and pass coverages.

A rookie may arrive at training camp with an All-American rating and a thick scrapbook of press clippings. He may be quick and have excellent speed. But coaches want to know, "Can he hit?" and "Will he hit?"

There are a number of different drills to determine who are the hitters. The best known is the nutcracker. An offensive lineman is pitted against a defensive man in a nine- or ten-foot space between two tackling dummies. A running back attempts to run through the "hole" created by the offensive man. Sometimes the nutcracker is expanded to include a linebacker and a second offensive man.

The nutcracker strips the game to its basics. It is offense vs. defense on a man-to-man basis. The hitters can be quickly recognized. So can the nonhitters. But the nutcracker also causes injuries. Some teams consider the drill too brutal and don't use it.

All teams feature scrimmages, however, with the white-shirted offensive unit pitted against the defensive units, usually attired in green shirts. Plays, formations, and coverages discussed in the meetings that day are drilled on. Besides the daytime meetings, there are also meetings several nights each week.

At 11:00 P.M. coaches make a bed check. Players are required to be in their rooms, or at least on the dorm floor. Absent players are fined. The amount usually begins at $50 and ranges upward, the exact amount depending on what time the man finally arrives.

When the New York Jets set up training camp in 1973, the team's linebacking corps was in a state of flux. Some veteran players had retired and injuries had also hurt. The Jets had drafted four linebackers the previous January and had taken on one other as a free agent. This made for a highly competitive situation, with twelve men vying for six or seven positions on the team roster.

Among the rookies was Bill Ferguson from San Diego State. His college coach described Ferguson as being "intelligent and dedicated," with "good range; a hard hitter." There was also rookie Bruce Bannon from Penn State. The scouting report on Bannon called him "an extremely smart player who makes few mistakes . . . very durable." Rookie Rob Spicer from Indiana was known for his "excellent pursuit." Joe Carbone from Delaware was described as being "a nasty, sadistic player."

White-shirted offensive team and coaches plot strategy.

Linebackers Al Atkinson (left) and Ralph Baker cover passes in Jet training session.

What's the difference between a rookie linebacker and a veteran? Physically, not much. Indeed, the rookie may be quicker and faster than the veteran.

But the man with pro experience is usually superior. "The veterans know what to expect in each formation," Bill Ferguson noted. "They recognize what's coming, which means they're better able to anticipate. That's the advantage they have.

"And it can be a big advantage. Being aggressive, having raw power and quickness—these things really don't mean a great deal if you go in the wrong direction, blow your coverage.

"The veteran player is less likely to make a mistake of this type. The coaches are confident in them as a result. They don't have the same confidence in a rookie player."

For the most part, a player's ability and his willingness to hit are determined on how he performs in preseason games. There are usually six of these. Rookies and other players of doubtful status ordinarily staff the special teams in these games—the kickoff and kickoff return team, the punt and punt return teams, and the field-goal and field-goal prevent team.

Preseason games are filmed, of course, and coaches study the films carefully and grade each man on the basis of his aggressiveness. "Get down there and knock the hell out of somebody on a punt," says one player, "and you can really impress people."

The names of players cut from the squad must be in the NFL office by Tuesday afternoon so that they can be circulated to other teams in the league. This means that teams usually make their cuts on Tuesday morning or Monday night.

During this time, players who are unsure of their jobs wait in fear of a visit from The Turk, the traditional name for the camp aide—sometimes it's an assistant equipment man, other times an assistant trainer—who knocks on the player's door and announces, "Coach wants to see you." Once the coach has told a player he's not going to make the team, he quickly packs and leaves.

There is much uncertainty about a career in pro football. But there is one thing almost every player can be sure of: sooner or later he is going to receive a visit from The Turk.

TWO OF THE BEST

Once after a game between the Colts and Bears in Chicago, the Baltimore team boarded their bus for the trip to the airport. They had not gone very far when a trailing automobile slammed into the bus from behind. "There's Butkus again," cracked one of the Baltimore players.

Butkus. The name even sounds tough. *But-kus*— two hard syllables, two shots from a pistol. *But-kus* —a left to the jaw, a right to the midsection.

Sport Magazine polled NFL quarterbacks not long ago, asking each which middle linebacker they feared the most. Characteristically, most said that they "feared" no one, but ten of the quarterbacks voted Butkus as being the best, and ten others classed him as one of the best. "The clear evidence," said *Sport*, "is that Dick Butkus remains king of the hill."

It's true—Dick Butkus was to linebacking what Babe Ruth was to baseball or Albert Einstein to theoretical physics. He is *the* linebacker of professional football.

Butkus was a big man—6-foot-3, 245 pounds. His size made him easy to pick out on the field. You noticed the huge shoulders, the wide expanse of chest, and the long arms. But it was not his size that made Butkus superior, it was his temperament.

As the kickoff drew near, he became more and more menacing. His face would be blank as he performed the warmup exercises. He ignored any opponent who might say "Hello," even if it happened to be an old college teammate.

Once the game began, Butkus was a man possessed. There was not a play he did not influence. He might not make the tackle or stop the pass, but he was there—rampaging right or left, striking out with his fists and forearms, hurling his body at the point of attack, shouting at the top of his lungs, always shouting.

Intimidating. That was the word for Dick Butkus. A quarterback had to think twice before sending a running play up the middle or passing into Butkus' zone. He inhibited the offense by his very presence. As one quarterback put it, "The best way to play Dick Butkus is to avoid him."

When the game was over and the players from both teams met in the center of the field, there would be much handshaking and backslapping. This was not for Butkus. No one said, "Nice game, Dick," and patted him on the fanny. Eyes straight ahead, his face grim, Butkus walked to the dressing room, and he walked alone. He was a man apart.

Coaches say that it takes two, maybe three years to learn to be a linebacker in professional football. You have to learn to read defenses. You have to learn your keys. It took Dick Butkus less than a season.

The Bears had intended that Butkus would be the No. 2 man behind middle linebacker Bill George for a season or two. But when George was slow in recovering from knee surgery, the Chicago coaches decided to give Butkus a try and let him learn from his mistakes.

The Bears lost their first three games and Butkus suffered many embarrassing moments. His pro debut is a game he'd like to forget. The Bears faced the 49ers and quarterback John Brodie put on a dazzling show, using draws and play-action to shred the Bear defenses. Time after time, Brodie sent San Francisco ball carriers up the middle through Butkus' territory for big gains. The final score saw the 49ers on top, 52-24, for the worst opening day defeat in Chicago history. Bear owner George Halas tried to make excuses for Butkus after the game, but it was obvious that Brodie had taken advantage of the raw rookie.

But little by little Butkus improved. Against the Vikings, he intercepted a pass and returned it 35 yards, setting up a touchdown that put the game out of reach. The following week in a game against the Lions, Butkus sparked a fired-up Chicago defense that caused five Detroit turnovers, and his teammates awarded him the game ball.

Late in November that season, the Bears flattened the Giants, 35-14, at Yankee Stadium, and Butkus picked off his fifth interception. Interviewed after the game, he said that he was beginning to feel

Dick Butkus takes the field.

91

comfortable with the intricate Chicago defenses. "It was a gradual learning process," he said, "but I'm beginning to get it down pat."

The Bears ended up winning nine of their last eleven games. Butkus led the team in both fumble recoveries and interceptions, so it wasn't exactly a surprise when he was named an All-NFL middle linebacker. The other All-NFL middle linebacker that season was Ray Nitschke. For Butkus, a rookie, to be classed with the great Nitschke was a sublime achievement.

Looking back, however, it isn't hard to understand. Playing football, professional football, was about the only thing that Dick Butkus ever wanted to do. It was almost an obsession.

Butkus was born in Chicago and raised there, one of eight children, the youngest of five boys. It was while in grade school, where he played fullback and linebacker, that he began aiming for a pro football career.

"Football is just what I've always wanted to do," says Butkus. "Some guys' goals change many times. Mine never did. I didn't like school one bit and I wanted to quit at first, but I went through with it because I knew that was how I could get to my goal."

When it came time to choose a high school, Butkus picked out Chicago Vocational, not because it was near his home, which it wasn't, and not because of its curriculum. It happened that Chicago Voca-

tional had a coach named Bernie O'Brien, who had played football at Notre Dame. Butkus had heard good things about him.

Butkus helped Chicago Vocational win a couple of public school championships and then accepted a scholarship offer from the University of Illinois. He had been such a standout performer in high school that he could have gone to just about any college he wanted, but he chose Illinois because it was close to home, and, being a member of the Big Ten, would offer top-flight competition.

"We knew from the first day he was a great one," said Pete Elliott, the Illinois coach. "Great" was the appropriate word. Besides winning All-American recognition in both 1963 and 1964, Butkus was named Lineman of the Year in 1965 and placed third in the voting for the Heisman Trophy (behind John Huarte of Notre Dame and Tucker Frederickson of Auburn).

From an academic standpoint, Butkus' career was not nearly so outstanding. "I wasn't ready for college," he once said. "I didn't have the background. I didn't have the study habits. My marks weren't any good, and if I hadn't made the pros and had to rely on my education for work, I would have been in trouble.

"Deep down, I just wanted to play pro ball, so I didn't care too much. But if I had to do it over again, I would work harder."

It didn't matter to pro football that Butkus had

It's a run, and Butkus wheels to meet it.

never made the dean's list. At the time he graduated, competition between the National Football League and the old American League had reached a fever pitch, and Butkus was the No. 1 draft choice of both the Chicago Bears and Denver Broncos. Chicago was where he wanted to play and the Bears knew it, so there wasn't a great deal of bidding for his services. Still, when he signed for an estimated $200,000 spread over four years, it represented the most money ever paid to a defensive player.

Abe Gibron, the Bears' coach, once described Butkus as being shy and withdrawn. "But then," says Gibron, "when the whistle blows, he sort of goes crazy.

"In my twenty-two years in the league, I've never seen a player with greater desire. Sometimes we literally have to pull him back in practice."

In a game against the Washington Redskins, Butkus spent much of the afternoon batting down Washington passes and hurling his body into the line to stop runs on vital third-down plays. One of his jolting tackles put Redskins' running back Charley Harraway out of the game.

Late in the final quarter, Cyril Pinder got free on a 40-yard touchdown run that pulled the Bears into a tie. The extra point would win it.

The teams lined up. Butkus, who blocked in the offensive backfield on conversion kicks, watched in dismay as the snap from center sailed over the kicker's head. As quarterback Bobby Douglass

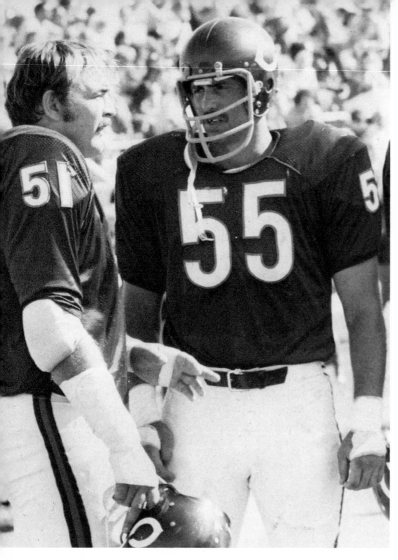

Butkus and colleague Doug Buffone

scrambled to retrieve the ball, Butkus, remembering that he was an eligible receiver, swung into the end zone. Douglass finally picked up the ball and when he scanned downfield looking for a receiver, there was Butkus waving his arms and screaming. The desperation throw was good and Butkus had scored the game-deciding point.

Butkus often served as a canny field general. In a game against the Minnesota Vikings, the Bears lined up for a field-goal attempt. Butkus, on the field to block, flashed a hand signal to coach Abe Gibron indicating he wanted to try a fake field goal. "Go ahead," Gibron signaled back.

After getting the word from Butkus, quarterback Bobby Douglass, who holds the ball on placements, called an audible announcing the fake. When the snap came back, Douglass scampered for a six-yard gain and a key first down.

Later in the same game, with the Bears in punt formation, Bobby Joe Green faked his kick, then threw a pass to Cecil Turner good for 23 yards and another first down. There were no hand signals this time. Butkus simply yelled, "Throw it, Bobby Joe! Throw it!"

Butkus also recovered a fumble in the game and intercepted a pass that led to the winning field goal. But after the game he seemed prouder of the fake-kick calls than anything else.

While Butkus was valued for his leadership qualities, it was for what he did physically that he is best known. Terry Bradshaw of the Steelers called Butkus "a thumb in the eye." The Lions' Greg Landry said that Butkus ". . . is so physical he can put the fear of God in you." Virgil Carter of the Bengals, once a teammate of Butkus, described him as being ". . . so intense that it's frightening."

"Ferocious" and "mean" are two other words used to describe Butkus. To the Detroit Lions, however, Butkus' conduct went beyond ordinary ferocity and meanness. Joe Schmidt, when he was the Detroit coach, once said of Butkus: "I never saw anything like him. He likes to hit guys. He's sadistic, bloodthirsty."

Schmidt had evidence. In one game, Charlie Sanders, the Lions' standout tight end, caught a pass and started to run with the ball. Butkus got his arms around Sanders and started crushing him with a bearhug, and when the whistle blew, Butkus kept right on squeezing. Sanders hardly had the strength to make the huddle. Later in the game, Sanders grabbed another pass, and this time Butkus poked his fingers through the bars of Sanders' facemask, threatening his eyeballs. The Lions managed to win the game, so Sanders could afford to be philosophical afterward. "Dick," he said, "is a maladjusted kid."

In another meeting of the two teams, Butkus whacked running back Altie Taylor with what looked to be a fierce karate chop to the helmet. The Detroit fans booed lustily. During the ensuing week,

95

Though big, Butkus is very agile.

when films of the game were shown to the Detroit team and the play rerun, the players booed.

Butkus defended his action. "I tried to rip the ball out of his hand," he said. "The fans thought I was trying to do something else. People get excited."

A reporter asked Taylor whether he was afraid of Butkus. "Afraid of him?" said Taylor. "Nah, I don't even realize he's out there until I hear the boos."

The two men continued to feud. In a game later that season, Taylor carried the ball on a sweep. As he neared the sidelines, Butkus drove his body into the smallish Taylor—and drove and drove. The two men catapulted into and through a cluster of sideline spectators seated on spindly metal chairs, and kept going until they smashed into a red brick wall that surrounded the playing field, with Butkus slamming Taylor into it.

There were jokes about Butkus, from people who say that he can't read without moving his lips, or that when he signs an autograph he writes an X. Being classed as something subhuman and being laughed at for it bothers Butkus, but not as much as it used to. He's come to realize that on the field in the heat of battle "you practically have to act like an animal. You're propelled by your baser instincts —hate and rage and the desire to inflict pain and punishment."

"Have you ever been scared on the football field?" Butkus was once asked.

"Scared?" he answered. "Scared of what?"

He thought for a minute. "Just injuries. That's the only thing to be afraid of. I'm always hurt. I've never really been healthy. If I ever felt really great and could play a hundred per cent, nobody'd know what was going on, I'd be so amazing."

Specifically, it was his knees that gave Butkus problems in recent years. He had knee surgery in January, 1971, and again in March that year. "I hurt the knee in high school," he once recalled, "and played four years. I hurt it in college—and played four more years. I played six years in the pros. So it was fourteen years with my knowing it was bad. I was on borrowed time."

To aid him in his recuperation, Butkus devoted countless hours to working out on the $2,400 worth of gym equipment that had been installed in his home two years before. As the opening of the season drew near, Butkus pronounced the knee sound. "It swung like a gate before," he said, "but now I can feel its tightness."

Some observers say that Dick Butkus was the last of his type, that he represents an era of defensive football that is beginning to fade. Middle line-backers of the future will be more noted for quickness and maneuverability, and will be able to cover on passes as well as they do on runs. No one argues that Butkus was better against the run than the pass. But he was so outstanding on runs that the quality of his pass protection *had* to suffer by comparison.

One man who typifies the "new" image is Mike Curtis of the Baltimore Colts. Curtis is fast. He's smooth. He does everything that's required of a middle linebacker and he does it with professional flair.

Curtis is a hitter, too. And when he hits, he drives his 6-foot-2-inch frame into the ball carrier with a terrible fury. It is generally agreed that, with the possible exception of Dick Butkus, no one punishes runners and receivers the way Mike Curtis does.

Even his teammates have learned to be a little bit wary of him. In practice sessions, Curtis had no qualms about slamming into quarterback Johnny Unitas, and the Colt veteran would get up muttering words that can't be repeated in a book to be read by young people. Unitas, before being dealt to the San Diego Chargers, was a Baltimore idol, the franchise. But not to Curtis. He played defense; Unitas played offense; he was the enemy. It was as simple as that.

What does Curtis say about himself, about being tagged with nicknames like The Animal and Mad Dog? "They say I go berserk on the field. Well, that's not exactly true. I've never tried to hurt anybody. I've never aimed for the legs or anything like that. It's just that I love contact.

"Football is the kind of a game in which you can express yourself in a physical way, when you can let it all go. I have my territory. I'm alone in that

Mike Curtis (right) and his former partner on the outside, Ray May.

territory. When someone comes into my territory, I'm going to get him and make him pay for trespassing on my turf."

Curtis didn't begin with the Colts as a linebacker. At Duke University, Mike was a running back, and a splendid one, establishing a career rushing record and winning at least one All-America honorable mention. He did some linebacking, too, but that was second in importance.

Not to the pro scouts, however. They felt he

Curtis hauls Jets' John Riggins to the ground.

should concentrate on being a linebacker. "A fierce tackler with fine pursuit," said a scouting report compiled by the New York Giants. "Could be an outstanding linebacker in the pros."

"I like his quickness," declared a scout for the Green Bay Packers. "He hits."

The Colts, having been manhandled in an NFL championship game by the Browns, 27-0, knew they had to bolster their defensive unit, so they went into the college draft in 1965 with the idea of getting a solid linebacker. They had their eyes on Dick Butkus of Illinois, but Butkus was picked off by the Bears. When it came Baltimore's turn to choose, Curtis was still available, so they "settled" for him.

Mike was very pleased. He had been born in Rockville, Maryland, and attended Richard Montgomery High School there, so it was a case of a local boy making good.

But Mike's pleasure at being named a member of the Colts quickly waned when he arrived at training camp that summer. In an off-season trade with the Lions, the Colts had obtained a seasoned linebacker in Dennis Gaubatz, and they had given up a running back to get him. The team no longer needed shoring up on defense. What they did need was help in the offensive backfield, and that's where they slotted Curtis.

Looking back, Curtis calls himself "a flop" as a pro running back. He had trouble finding the holes and making cuts, and one of his teammates recalls that he wobbled when he ran with the ball.

It was a disappointing year for the young man and the next season began in much the same fashion. Before it was very old, Mike hurt a knee returning a kick. This ended the Colts' ambitions of making a running back out of him. Mike was assigned to the linebacking unit. In the first game he started, he led the team in tackles, as the Colts trounced the Lions, 45-14. His teammates awarded Mike the game ball.

He still had much to learn, however. Sometimes he lined up wrong and occasionally he'd fail to cover the area he was supposed to cover. Then, in his anxiety to atone for the error, and make the tackle, he'd sometimes accidentally trample one of his teammates. Yet the coaches could see his potential. "Curtis has an instinct for the ball that can't be taught," said linebacker coach Chuck Noll, later to be the head coach of the Steelers. "He'll keep improving."

One thing that hampered Mike's improvement was his knee, the one he had injured the year before. When he hurt it again in 1967, he had to submit to surgery. He played only three games that season, but when he returned to the lineup in 1968 he was better than ever. "I spent the year I was hurt learning how to think the way a linebacker is supposed to think," he said. And he worked on improving his quickness—to react more quickly, to move more quickly. "Get the job done," he says. "Get it done quick. Get it done quicker. Get it done the quickest."

Curtis established himself as one of pro football's premiere linebackers that season, winning All-Pro honors. One game that year stands out in his memory. Unfortunately, it was a losing game; more unfortunately, it was the Super Bowl.

The Colts had won 15 of 16 games and ranked as the best defensive team in football, bar none. But the Jets' Joe Namath victimized the Baltimore defense with his quick, pinpoint passes. Mike himself looks back upon the ordeal in horror.

He recalls one play in which the Colts blitzed. A back swung out to Curtis' side—he was a corner linebacker then—and it was his job to cover the man, but Mike was intent upon blitzing and flattening Joe Namath, the Colts' tormentor, and he forgot his assignment. Namath cooly lopped the ball over Mike's head for an 8-yard gain. "I stood there feeling like a jerk," Mike said afterward. "It was the biggest mental mistake I ever made." Mike wasn't the only one to make mental mistakes that day, and the Colts were dumped, 16-7.

Curtis liked playing for Don Shula, who coached the Colts until he departed for the Miami Dolphins in 1970. Under Shula's system, the linebackers, indeed, all members of the defensive unit, played under a tight rein. You did your job. There was little chance to be creative. But Curtis found no fault with this. "I like Shula's discipline," he once said. "In fact, I love it. I believe in discipline. If you're going to be consistent, you have to have it.

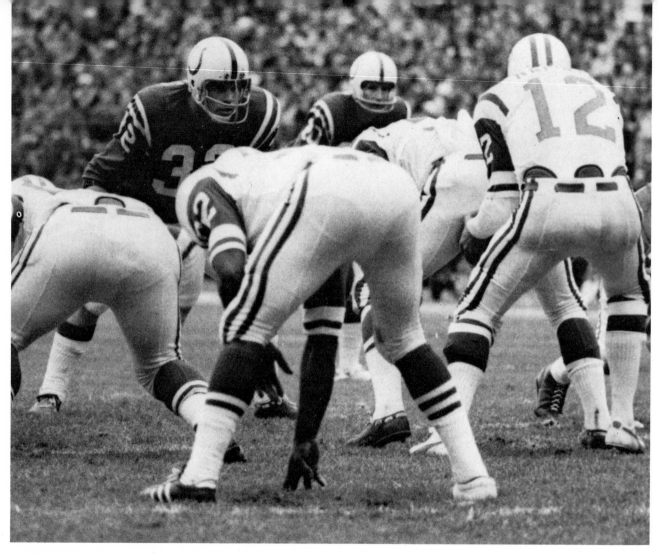

Curtis glares as Joe Namath calls signals.

"The idea of men-are-men, treat-them-like-men is all wrong. It doesn't make sense. Some men are going to take responsibility and some aren't.

"If I were a coach, I'd be like [General] Patton." Curtis once disclosed that he had seen the movie based on Patton's life six times. "I'd want my players to be as obedient as Patton's soldiers."

Curtis' high regard for Shula may have dimmed somewhat in recent years. Not long after Shula had taken over in Miami, the Colts faced the Dolphins in the Orange Bowl. Early in the second quarter, quarterback Bob Griese rolled out to his right looking for a receiver, and when he couldn't find one he sprinted toward the sidelines. He never made it. Curtis came roaring up to belt Griese to the ground, using his right hand and forearm, which happened to be enclosed in a padded cast. The officials called it unnecessary roughness and penalized the Colts 15 yards.

Later in the game, another play brought Curtis near the Dolphins' bench where Shula was standing. The two men went at one another bitterly. "I don't know who spoke first," Shula said later, "but what was said was unprintable."

Curtis defended his actions. "He [Griese] was in bounds," Curtis said. "When he's running he's fair game to get his head knocked off. That's what this game is all about." Because the officials had levied a penalty against the Colts, he accused them of "pussycat stuff."

Curtis is a conservative in his social and political values, and that is putting it mildly. "Anyone who calls a policeman a pig should be shot," he says. He will tell you that he doesn't like "liberal, emancipated women," New York City, permissiveness, black militancy, Big Government, welfare, the writings of Bernie Parrish, Dave Meggyesy and Jim Bouton, unions and union leaders. Curtis' own union, the NFL Players' Association, is no exception. When the Players' Association went on strike in 1970, Curtis was the only regular player in the NFL to report to training camp on time. In other words, he crossed the picket line. Later he quit the organization.

The Colts got back into the Super Bowl in January, 1971. This time they opposed the Dallas Cowboys. Mike and his teammates looked forward to vindicating themselves for what had happened two years before.

With less than two minutes to play and the score tied, 13-13, Dallas had possession on the Baltimore 48-yard line. On first down, Duane Thomas was thrown for a one-yard loss. Then Craig Morton, back to throw, was crumpled to the ground for a 9-yard loss. A holding penalty cost the Cowboys fifteen more yards. Now Morton was desperate. Once more he went back to pass, this time targeting on running back Dan Reeves. As Reeves stepped in front of the ball to make the catch, safety Jerry Logan piled into him from behind. The ball popped

Curtis gets congratulations following a pass interception.

up into the air, and when it came down, Curtis, who had raced over from the opposite side of the field, was there to make the catch. He streaked 13 yards to the Dallas 28-yard line before being tackled.

Quarterback Earl Morrall called two running plays to use up the clock. Then Jim O'Brien came in to kick the winning field goal.

Everyone agreed that Curtis' interception was the game's turning point. But there was also a fairly unanimous feeling that the game was something less than an artistic triumph. Indeed, it was a zany affair, with no less than eleven turnovers resulting from interceptions and fumbles. But Curtis and his teammates on the Colt defensive unit attributed the turnovers to their punishing play. Mike called it a "good physical game," and Jerry Logan said there had been "some great defensive football." It doesn't matter how you appraise the contest aesthetically. What does matter is that the record book will always say: Colts, 16; Dallas, 13.

After Baltimore's win in Super Bowl V, troubled seasons followed. A new owner took over and a new general manager in Joe Thomas.

Thomas completed almost two dozen trades in 1972 and 1973 in his effort to renovate the team. He was beseiged with offers for Curtis, but each was greeted with a loud "No."

The great Johnny Unitas could be dispatched to San Diego, superstar Bubba Smith could be dealt to Oakland, and other Colt stars wound up all over the football map. But Mike Curtis stayed in Baltimore. To Thomas he was untouchable.

Jack Ham

PLAYING THE OUTSIDE

In an American Conference play-off game in 1972, quarterback Daryle Lamonica of the Oakland Raiders thought he saw a flaw in the Pittsburgh Steelers' pass defense. On the next play, he sent ace receiver Fred Biletnikoff on a quick square-out pattern. Biletnikoff never got a chance to touch the ball. Linebacker Jack Ham darted up to make an interception.

Later in the game, Lamonica attempted to bring the sputtering Oakland offense to life by sending Biletnikoff sprinting downfield on a long "go" pattern. Ham picked him up, then matched him stride for stride, and when Lamonica's long throw came earthward Ham batted it away.

There are few linebackers better than Jack Ham when it comes to covering on passes. He has the quickness to be able to stop the short ones and the speed of a cornerback when covering deep. Nick Skorich, coach of the Cleveland Browns, says that Ham is "so intuitive that you just have to get the jump on him. If you can't get him out of position, he's going to hurt you."

Ham "hurt" a large number of people in 1972, his second season in pro football. He led all linebackers in interceptions with seven, and one of the steals, against the Patriots, Ham turned into a touchdown, the first of his career.

A friendly, down-to-earth young man, Jack Ham

is regarded as one of the best outside linebackers in the game. Dave Robinson of the Redskins and Ted Hendricks of the Colts, who are also profiled in this chapter, are two others who excel.

How do you judge the performance of an outside linebacker? One good way is to watch a running back as he swings out for a pass. The outside linebacker should be there to make the play, darting up to cover.

When the offensive team runs a sweep, it's the outside linebacker's job to force the play in toward the middle. He may get obliterated doing it, but that's all in a day's work. He's also responsible for running plays that veer to his side of the line, in which case he must charge forward, throw aside the blocker, and make the tackle.

The tight end is another responsibility that the outside linebacker has. Since the tight end usually lines up on the right side, it's the linebacker on the left who must control him. Quarterbacks are finding that it's increasingly difficult to complete long passes to their wide receivers because of the growing sophistication of zone defenses. As a result, they're targeting with greater frequency on the tight ends, a fact that any outside linebacker will substantiate.

Jack Ham has been playing outside linebacker since his prep school days. An All-American at Penn State and the team's defensive captain, Ham was the Steelers' No. 2 draft choice in 1971. Pittsburgh

Ham confers with defensive coordinator Bud Carson.

coach Chuck Noll was asked why he placed such a high estimate on Ham's skills, when there were so many more-glittering prospects available. "He makes the big play," Noll answered. "He makes things happen—interceptions, recoveries, forcing fumbles, blocking kicks. He gets you the ball. Even though he's on defense, he's an offensive threat."

Ham, who lives in Pittsburgh and works for the City Department of Parks and Recreation, could well have ended up as a playground director, getting his football on television. At Bishop McCort High School in Johnstown, Pennsylvania, Ham was a lineman, but an infrequent one, not getting into any games until the middle of his senior year. He was not surprised when he did not win any scholarship offers.

But Ham was young, only sixteen, so his father suggested a year of prep school. Jack signed up at Massanutten Military Academy, in nearby Virginia. Although he distinguished himself on the football team there, no college came forward with a scholarship. Jack then decided to enroll at Penn State as a plain, ordinary student.

But a teammate of his from Bishop McCort, who had gone directly to Penn State, had been selling coach Joe Paterno on Ham's merits. Shortly before the school term began, a scholarship became available. Paterno told Ham's friend, "O.K., you win. Bring him in. We'll find out if we have a football player."

Ham's prep school coach had gotten him to switch to linebacker, so as to take advantage of his speed and mobility. "I was more confident, too," says Ham. "I knew I could hold my own. I don't know if I would have felt like that a year earlier, when I was sixteen." Ham became a starter as a sophomore and began winning All-America recognition as a junior. He starred in the 1969 and 1970 Orange Bowl games.

Ham greeted the news that he had been selected by the Steelers with mixed emotions. The team's record had been 1-13 and 5-9 in the two preceding seasons. Ham was used to playing with a winner. Besides, Ham had hoped his athletic career might get him out of Pennsylvania. "I had lived all my life in Johnstown and then went to Penn State," he once recalled. "The thought of playing pro ball in Pittsburgh didn't fit my idea of becoming a well-traveled athlete."

But Ham's disenchantment quickly turned to bliss. Veterans Chuck Allen and Andy Russell, two of the team's regular linebackers, made a special effort to help Ham learn the Pittsburgh defensive system. "Allen and Russell were real pros," Ham recalls. "They went out of their way to make things easy for me."

A word about Andy Russell, Ham's partner on the other side. Quick and sure, one of the smartest linebackers in the league, Russell won All-Rookie honors in 1963 and has been an All-Pro choice many times since. He has been the Steelers' defensive captain since 1967.

The camaraderie helped Ham overcome any misgivings he might have had about the Steelers, but

Andy Russell

just as important was the fact that the team started winning. In 1972 they won so frequently that they ended up in the AFC championship game, only to lose to the Miami Dolphins, the eventual Super Bowl champion.

Ham isn't big—6-foot-2, 220 pounds—but he is fast and has hair-trigger reactions. "Coaches want mobility now, not size," says Andy Russell. "The emphasis is on pass coverage, not stopping the run."

Ham has been so successful at batting down passes and making interceptions that, as Philadelphia sportswriter Jack McKinney once noted, his coverage statistics look like those of a free safety. When Ham was asked how he managed to achieve such success, he gave four reasons: L. C. Greenwood, Joe Greene, Ben McGee, and Dwight White —the Pittsburgh front four. "When you work behind the kind of rush those guys give you up front," he said, "you feel free to take chances, to go for the big play."

The Steelers' supporters are among the most ardent in the NFL. Fan clubs abound. Ham can attest to the enthusiam. He was once given an ovation during a church service. It happened in 1972, the Steelers' glory year. Ham was in the congregation one Sunday as the pastor sermonized on parish affairs, when suddenly he switched topics to proclaim, "How about those Steelers!" Then he asked whether Dan Rooney, an official of the team and a member of the parish, was present. Rooney wasn't,

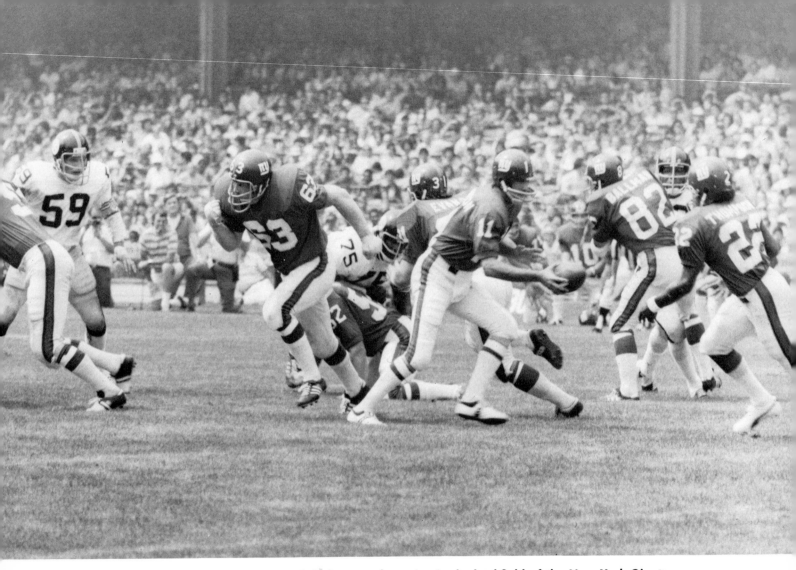

Is it a pass or a run? Ham (extreme left) keys on the action in the backfield of the New York Giants.

but since Ham was there he stood up. "They gave me a big ovation," Ham recalls, "just like at the stadium. After Mass I stayed around and signed autographs."

The Redskins' Dave Robinson has never received the acclaim of a church congregation, but it happens to be one of the few honors he hasn't won. Originally drafted by the Green Bay Packers in the first round of the 1963 college draft, Robinson was a Packer regular for ten years before going to the 'Skins. He was named the NFL's Most Valuable Lineman in 1968, and he has gone to the Pro Bowl three times. Like Joe Schmidt and Ray Nitschke, Robinson can be termed a "great" linebacker.

"He has exceptionally good hands, good speed, and he's a hard tackler," Henry Jordan, an All-NFL tackle and a teammate of Robinson at Green Bay, once said. "What makes a linebacker successful is being able to analyze the play and react quickly, and, if it's a run, to fill the hole. If it's a pass, he must go deep. Dave can do all that."

During the years that Robinson was with the Packers, they were pro football's most formidable team. Robinson was one reason they held that ranking. Time after time in championship games, it was he who made *the* crucial defensive play. When the Packers faced the Colts with the Western Division title at stake in December, 1965, Green Bay held a slight edge, 14-13, with time running out in the first half. Quarterback Gary Cuozzo marched the

Dave Robinson

109

Colts to the Packer 2-yard line.

There was less than a minute to play as the teams lined up. As the ball was snapped, Robinson read run, and the fact that tight end John Mackey was barreling toward him confirmed his expectations. But suddenly Mackey released, and out of the corner of his eye Robinson caught a glimpse of the fullback swinging out of the end zone. "Oh, oh—pass," thought Robinson, and started pedaling back.

Cuozzo tried to loop the ball over Robinson's head but he failed to get it high enough. Dave reached up and made the catch, then sprinted 87 yards to the Baltimore 10-yard line. A touchdown quickly followed. The Packers, instead of trailing, 20-14, went off the field with a 21-13 lead. "It was a 14-point play; it was the turning point," said Packer coach Vince Lombardi afterward.

Robinson also made vital contributions the next year in the Western Conference championship and the NFL title game, both won by Green Bay.

Always an aggressive player, Robinson had no trouble getting psyched up for games. He reasons like this: Going to the Super Bowl and winning it is worth about $25,000 to each man, or about $1,000 per game (counting the preseason games). "I treat the opposition," he says, "the same way that I'd treat a common thief I found in my house trying to steal my money. What would you do," he asked, "if you found a thief helping himself to $1,000 of your money? How would you act?"

A torn Achilles' tendon ruined Robinson's 1970 season and hindered him in 1971. But 1972 was different. Before the season opened, coach Dan Devine of the Packers said that the team's success on defense depended on how well Robinson played. Well, the team finished No. 1 in defense in the NFC, and the Packers ended up—surprisingly—in the Conference play-offs.

Robinson had also been successful as a business executive, so successful, in fact, that he decided to retire from pro football in 1972. He announced he was quitting about the same time that the Packers made it known they had traded him to Washington.

Redskin coach George Allen said he wanted Robinson "because he doesn't make mistakes. He'll smell out the play-action pass. Robinson knows when to commit, and when to fall off to get that running back who's usually the target on play-action."

Allen also lauded Robinson for his ability "to string a play out," explaining that "Robinson uses his hands to fence with the blockers if it's a run. They don't get to his legs. He can also shed a running guard and often brings down a runner by himself. If he doesn't make the tackle, he's stringing out the other team's running play, giving our defense time to get into action."

Early in 1973, Allen got Robinson to change his mind about retiring. Actually, Allen didn't have to do too much selling. "As we got closer and closer to

Robinson has a fist for Buffalo's tight end John Mosier.

the season," said Robinson, "I got to feeling more and more like a football player and less and less like an executive."

In the Washington scheme of things, Robinson lined up on the left side, leaving the right in the capable hands of Chris Hanburger. A strong blitzer and outstanding in covering any type of pass, Hanburger was voted the NFC's Defensive Player of the Year in 1972. As middle linebacker, the Redskins had veteran Myron Pottios, who had been chosen for the Pro Bowl three times.

Robinson, Hanburger, and Pottios comprised a linebacking trio that was regarded by many as the best in pro football. But challenges in that regard came from the Baltimore Colts, who could boast Mike Curtis as their middle linebacker and Ray May and Ted Hendricks at the corners.

Hendricks, who plays the left side, is special. What makes him special is his speed, strength, and size, mostly the latter. Hendricks is 6-foot-7, 220 pounds.

Attempting to throw a football over the up-stretched arms of a 6-foot-7 linebacker is not the kind of situation any quarterback likes to contemplate. As Baltimore coach Howard Schnellenberger has said, "Hendricks introduced a concept in linebacking unlike almost any other in pro ball. He creates a completely different problem for the quarterback."

Quarterback Bob Davis of the New York Jets

Above: Ted Hendricks *Right:* Chris Hanburger

(later traded to the New Orleans Saints) would agree. Once in a game against the Colts, the Jets were leading, 7-0, and Davis had the team on the move. But Hendricks intercepted one of Davis' passes. The Colts tied the game and then went on to win.

In the locker room afterward, Davis talked about the interception. "I knew there was a linebacker between me and the receiver," he said, "but I've thrown over them before and didn't expect any trouble doing it this time.

"It's just that you don't have any time to think that it's Ted Hendricks and he's 6-foot-7. All of a sudden he leaps straight up in the air like a basketball player and turns the game around."

Like any of the better linebackers, Hendricks reacts quickly. He studies opposition players carefully, classifying quarterbacks as pointers and nonpointers. "A pointer," he explains, "is a quarterback who looks right where he is going to throw all the time he's dropping back. You just go where he's pointing.

"It's harder if the passer looks off one way and then comes back the other. Then you have to figure out the pattern.

"Suppose they send the wide receiver to the outside on a curl pattern and keep the back in to block. I know there's nobody going to hurt me on the inside, so I don't stand around. I got out there where the receiver is."

Hendricks is also outstanding when it comes to stopping running plays. "I usually like to hit the ball carrier high, up around the waist," he says. "It's easier for me to make a high tackle than go low and probably miss."

He keeps blockers away from him just with his hands. "Most of them really don't want to come in too low," he says. "When they do that, they can miss altogether, so most of them try to stay high."

Hendricks was a three-time All-American at the University of Miami, not as a linebacker, but as a defensive end and tight end. He was the Colts' No. 2 draft pick in 1969, but when he arrived at camp that summer the coaches were uncertain as to where to start him. Players who stand 6-foot-7 and weigh 220 pounds are as rare as left-handed quarterbacks, rarer, in fact. At first they thought of Hendricks as a defensive end, and they issued him jersey number 83 (which he still wears), a defensive end's number. Later they switched him to outside linebacker, where his competition was Mike Curtis, a four-year veteran at the position.

Curtis didn't make it easy for rookie Hendricks. "He wouldn't even let me practice," Ted once recalled. "I'd go in and two plays later Mike would come running out and chase me off the field. He'd say he needed the work."

In November of that year, with the Colts struggling to stay in contention, coach Don Shula made some changes. He switched Curtis to middle line-

backer in place of Dennis Gaubatz. Ray May took over Curtis' slot on the right side, and Hendricks was inserted on the left. The combination was one of the Colts' basic strengths for years.

Hendricks had a super year in 1971, when he was a unanimous All-Pro selection. In his first Pro Bowl, he intercepted one of Roger Staubach's passes to set up a field goal.

Hendricks' elongated appearance and his aggressiveness on the field have earned him the nickname "The Mad Stork." He's not very happy about it, but he figures it's better than the nickname he had in college. There he was known as "Twiggy."

Opposite: **Hendricks (83) prefers to tackle high.**

NATIONAL FOOTBALL LEAGUE—ALL-LEAGUE LINEBACKERS

1952
Chuck Bednarik, Philadelphia Eagles (AP, UP)
Jerry Shipkey, Pittsburgh Steelers (AP)
George Connor, Chicago Bears (UP)

1953
Chuck Bednarik, Philadelphia Eagles (AP)
Don Paul, Los Angeles Rams (UP)
Tommy Thompson, Cleveland Browns (UP)
Tommy Keane, Baltimore Colts (AP, UP)

1954
Chuck Bednarik, Philadelphia Eagles (AP, UP)
Joe Schmidt, Detroit Lions (AP)
Roger Zatkoff, Green Bay Packers (UP)

1955
Chuck Bednarik, Philadelphia Eagles (UP)
George Connor, Chicago Bears (UP)
Joe Schmidt, Detroit Lions (AP)
Roger Zatkoff, Green Bay Packers (AP)

1956
Chuck Bednarik, Philadelphia Eagles (UP)
Les Richter, Los Angeles Rams (AP)
Joe Schmidt, Detroit Lions (AP, UP)

1957
Bill George, Chicago Bears (AP, UP)

Marv Matuszak, San Francisco 49ers (AP, UP)
Joe Schmidt, Detroit Lions (AP, UP)

1958
Bill George, Chicago Bears (AP, UPI)
Sam Huff, New York Giants (AP, UPI)
Joe Schmidt, Detroit Lions (AP, UPI)

1959
Bill George, Chicago Bears (AP, UPI)
Sam Huff, New York Giants (AP, UPI)
Joe Schmidt, Detroit Lions (AP, UPI)

1960
Chuck Bednarik, Philadelphia Eagles (AP, UPI)
Bill Forester, Green Bay Packers (AP, UPI)
Bill George, Chicago Bears (AP, UPI)

1961
Dan Currie, Green Bay Packers (NEA, UPI)
Bill George, Chicago Bears (AP, NEA)
Bill Forester, Green Bay Packers (AP, UPI)
Joe Schmidt, Detroit Lions (AP, NEA, UPI)

1962
Middle Linebacker
Joe Schmidt, Detroit Lions (AP, NEA, UPI)

Outside Linebacker
Dan Currie, Green Bay Packers (AP, NEA, UPI)
Bill Forester, Green Bay Packers (AP, NEA, UPI)

1963
Middle Linebacker
Bill George, Chicago Bears (AP, UPI)
Joe Schmidt, Detroit Lions (NEA)

Outside Linebacker
Joe Fortunato, Chicago Bears (AP, NEA, UPI)
Bill Forester, Green Bay Packers (UPI)
Jack Pardee, Los Angeles Rams (AP)
Myron Pottios, Pittsburgh Steelers (NEA)

1964
Middle Linebacker
Ray Nitschke, Green Bay Packers (AP, UPI)
Dale Meinert, St. Louis Cardinals (NEA)

Outside Linebacker
Maxie Baughan, Philadelphia Eagles (AP)
Joe Fortunato, Chicago Bears (AP, NEA, UPI)
Jim Houston, Cleveland Browns (NEA)
Wayne Walker, Detroit Lions (UPI)

1965
Middle Linebacker
Dick Butkus, Chicago Bears (AP, NEA)
Ray Nitschke, Green Bay Packers (UPI)

Outside Linebacker
Wayne Walker, Detroit Lions (AP, NEA, UPI)

Joe Fortunato, Chicago Bears (AP, NEA)
Jim Houston, Cleveland Browns (UPI)

1966
Middle Linebacker
Ray Nitschke, Green Bay Packers (AP, NEA, UPI)

Outside Linebacker
Chuck Howley, Dallas Cowboys (AP, NEA, UPI)
Lee Roy Caffey, Green Bay Packers (AP, UPI)
Maxie Baughan, Los Angeles Rams (NEA)

1967
Middle Linebacker
Dick Butkus, Chicago Bears (NEA, UPI)
Tommy Nobis, Atlanta Falcons (AP)

Outside Linebacker
Maxie Baughan, Los Angeles Rams (UPI)
Chuck Howley, Dallas Cowboys (AP)
Dave Robinson, Green Bay Packers (AP, NEA, UPI)
Dave Wilcox, San Francisco 49ers (NEA)

1968
Dick Butkus, Chicago Bears (AP, NEA, UPI)
Mike Curtis, Baltimore Colts (AP, UPI)
Chuck Howley, Dallas Cowboys (AP, NEA)
Dave Robinson, Green Bay Packers (NEA, UPI)

1969
Dick Butkus, Chicago Bears (AP, NEA, UPI)
Chuck Howley, Dallas Cowboys (AP, NEA, UPI)
Dave Robinson, Green Bay Packers (AP, NEA, UPI)

1970

Middle Linebacker
Dick Butkus, Chicago Bears (PFWA)

Outside Linebacker
Bobby Bell, Kansas City Chiefs (PFWA)
Chuck Howley, Dallas Cowboys (PFWA)

1971

Middle Linebacker
Willie Lanier, Kansas City Chiefs (PFWA)

Outside Linebacker
Ted Hendricks, Baltimore Colts (PFWA)
Dave Wilcox, San Francisco 49ers (PFWA)

1972

Middle Linebacker
Dick Butkus, Chicago Bears (NEA, PFWA)

Outside Linebacker
Chris Hanburger, Washington Redskins (NEA, PFWA)
Dave Wilcox, San Francisco 49ers (NEA, PFWA)

1973

Middle Linebacker
Lee Roy Jordan, Dallas Cowboys (NEA, PFWA)

Outside Linebacker
Chris Hanburger, Washington Redskins (NEA)
Isiah Robertson, Los Angeles Rams (PFWA)
Dave Wilcox, San Francisco 49ers (NEA, PFWA)

(Key to abbreviations: AP, Associated Press; NEA, Newspaper Enterprise Association; PFWA, Pro Football Writers of America; UP, United Press; and UPI, United Press International)

AMERICAN FOOTBALL LEAGUE—ALL-LEAGUE LINEBACKERS

1960
Archie Matsos, Buffalo Bills
Sherrill Headrick, Dallas Texans
Tom Addison, Boston Patriots

1961
Chuck Allen, San Diego Chargers
Sherrill Headrick, Dallas Texans
Archie Matsos, Buffalo Bills

1962
Middle Linebacker
Sherrill Headrick, Dallas Texans

Corner Linebackers
Larry Grantham, New York Titans
E. J. Holub, Dallas Texans

1963
Middle Linebacker
Archie Matsos, Buffalo Bills

Corner Linebackers
Tom Addison, Boston Patriots
E. J. Holub, Kansas City Chiefs

1964
Middle Linebacker
Nick Buoniconti, Boston Patriots

Corner Linebackers
Tom Addison, Boston Patriots
Larry Grantham, New York Jets

1965
Middle Linebacker
Nick Buoniconti, Boston Patriots

Corner Linebackers
Bobby Bell, Kansas City Chiefs
Mike Stratton, Buffalo Bills

1966
Middle Linebacker
Nick Buoniconti, Boston Patriots

Corner Linebackers
Bobby Bell, Kansas City Chiefs
Mike Stratton, Buffalo Bills

1967
Middle Linebacker
Nick Buoniconti, Boston Patriots

Corner Linebackers
Bobby Bell, Kansas City Chiefs
George Webster, Houston Oilers

1968

Middle Linebacker
Willie Lanier, Kansas City Chiefs

Outside Linebackers
Bobby Bell, Kansas City Chiefs
George Webster, Houston Oilers

1969

Middle Linebacker
Nick Buoniconti, Miami Dolphins

Outside Linebackers
Bobby Bell, Kansas City Chiefs
George Webster, Houston Oilers

(Teams from 1960-1966 were selected on the basis of player voting. From 1967-1969, selections were a consensus of choices from those made by the Associated Press, United Press International, Newspaper Enterprise Association and *The Sporting News.*)

INDEX